VIRGINIA TRIVIA

REVISED EDITION

VIRGINIA TRIVIA

**COMPILED BY
ERNIE & JILL COUCH**

REVISED EDITION

Rutledge Hill Press
Nashville, Tennessee

Published by Rutledge Hill Press, Inc., 211 Seventh Avenue North,
Nashville, Tennessee 37219

Typography by ProtoType Graphics, Inc.
and Bailey Typography, Inc.

Library of Congress Cataloging-in-Publication Data

Couch, Ernie, 1949–
    Virginia trivia/compiled by Ernie & Jill Couch. — Rev. ed.
      p.   cm.
    ISBN 1-55853-139-4
    1. Virginia — Miscellanea.   2. Questions and answers. 1. Couch.
Jill, 1948-   II. Title.
    F226.5.C68   1991
    975.5 — dc20   91-36305
                                                CIP

Printed in the United States of America
4 5 6 7 8 — 96 95 94

PREFACE

When *Virginia Trivia* was originally compiled, it became evident that many volumes could be written about this fascinating state. Virginia has a colorful and compelling history based on a richly diversified land and people. Now the revised edition of *Virginia Trivia* captures even more interesting facts about this exciting heritage.

Virginia Trivia is designed to be informative, educational, and entertaining. Most of all we hope that you will be motivated to learn even more about the great state of Virginia.

Ernie & Jill Couch

To the Cains
and
the great people of Virginia

TABLE OF CONTENTS

GEOGRAPHY

C H A P T E R   O N E

Q. The Indian name *Shenandoah* has what meaning?

A. "Daughter of the stars."

Q. What was the first road between Jamestown and Williamsburg named?

A. The Iron Bound Road.

Q. Near what city did Virginia's "tea party," similar to the Boston Harbor event, take place?

A. Yorktown.

Q. What is the length of Virginia's tidal shoreline?

A. 1,280 miles.

Q. At the beginning of World War I, what was the richest town per capita in the nation?

A. Reedville.

Q. What are the largest religious groups in Virginia?

A. Southern Baptists and Methodists.

Q. What municipality founded by the English is the oldest in existence in the United States?

A. Hampton.

Q. Charles O'Hara built what Petersburg dwelling utilizing no right angles to avoid having ghosts live with him?

A. Trapezium House.

Q. What is Virginia's eastern seaboard generally called?

A. Tidewater.

Q. Where was General Stonewall Jackson born on January 21, 1824?

A. Clarksburg, now in West Virginia.

Q. By what early name was Accomac known?

A. Drummond.

Q. What is the length of the gubernatorial term in Virginia?

A. Four years.

Q. The John W. Flannagan Dam and Reservoir is on what river?

A. Pound River.

———◆———

Q. Where did Lord De La Warr's supply ships overtake beleaguered colonists and encourage their return to Jamestown?

A. Mulberry Island.

———◆———

Q. What Virginia city is known internationally as the largest shipbuilder in the world?

A. Newport News.

———◆———

Q. Tappahannock, seat of Essex County, has what Indian meaning?

A. "On the Rising Waters."

———◆———

Q. What is the second oldest continuously used courthouse in the United States?

A. Hanover County Courthouse.

———◆———

Q. The headwaters of the Bullpasture and Cowpasture rivers form in what county?

A. Highland.

———◆———

Q. Dies for postmarking U.S. mail were manufactured by Chamber Engraving Company in what community from 1877 to 1928?

A. Lodge, near Callao.

Q. After having been accidentally shot by his own troops, General Stonewall Jackson was brought to what community where he died on May 10, 1863?

A. Guinea Station.

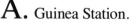

Q. Where was Patrick Henry born?

A. Studley, Hanover County.

Q. Approximately how many acres comprise Arlington National Cemetery?

A. 612.

Q. What famous Virginia mother lived the last part of her life at 1200 Charles Street, Fredericksburg?

A. Mary Washington, mother of George Washington.

Q. Clifford was incorporated in 1785 under what name?

A. Cabellsburg.

Q. What is the largest canyon east of the Mississippi River?

A. Breaks Interstate Canyon.

Q. Where is William Atkinson Jones, who campaigned for the independence of the Philippines, buried?

A. Warsaw.

Q. Chincoteague Island is the gateway to what national sea-shore?

A. Assateague Island National Seashore.

Q. What Wise County town was first named Prince's Flats in honor of Prince William?

A. Norton.

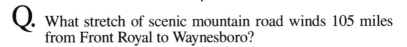

Q. Martha Dandridge, who later became the first first lady, was born at Chestnut Grove estate near what community on June 2, 1731?

A. New Kent.

Q. How many U.S. presidents were born in Virginia?

A. Eight.

Q. What stretch of scenic mountain road winds 105 miles from Front Royal to Waynesboro?

A. Skyline Drive.

Q. A tour of what community includes the office used by George Washington while surveying land for Lord Fairfax in 1756?

A. Winchester.

Q. Before changing its name to honor Confederate general J. E. B. Stuart, by what name was the town of Stuart called?

A. Taylorsville.

Q. Because of the pottery industry that flourished in Strasburg during the 1800s, what nickname did the town receive?

A. "Pot Town."

Q. On what Richmond thoroughfare do statues of J. E. B. Stuart and Stonewall Jackson face the north while a statue of Robert E. Lee faces south?

A. Monument Avenue.

Q. Where was Woodrow Wilson born?

A. Staunton.

Q. Where does Virginia rank in area among the states?

A. Thirty-sixth.

Q. What northern Virginia plantation did George Washington give to his wife Martha's granddaughter, Eleanor Parke Custis, and his nephew, Lawrence Lewis, as a wedding present?

A. Woodlawn Plantation, Mount Vernon.

Q. Governor John Garland Pollard, who served Virginia from 1930 to 1934, was born at the Bunker Hill house in what community?

A. Stevensville.

Q. What community and county were named in honor of William and Mary?

A. King and Queen.

Q. What fort was erected near Cherrydale during the War Between the States?

A. Fort Ethan Allen.

Q. Thoroughfare Gap is in what mountains?

A. The Bull Run Mountains.

Q. Having four churches on its short main street led to the choice of what name for an Augusta County Town in the 1800s?

A. Churchville.

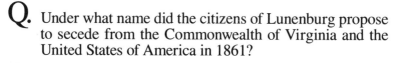

Q. Where is the state capital of Virginia?

A. Richmond.

Q. Under what name did the citizens of Lunenburg propose to secede from the Commonwealth of Virginia and the United States of America in 1861?

A. The Old Free State.

Q. Front Royal was called by what name before being chartered in 1788?

A. Hell Town.

Q. What county was the tobacco capital of the nation in the early 1800s because of its many factories?

A. Pittsylvania.

Q. What three Virginia communities are called the "Historic Triangle"?

A. Jamestown, Williamsburg, and Yorktown.

Q. Former Associate justice of the U.S. Supreme Court, Lewis Franklin Powell, Jr., was born in what Virginia community?

A. Suffolk.

Q. How many consecutive terms may a governor of Virginia serve?

A. None.

Q. Oak Hill Farm, Aldie, was the home of what Virginia-born U.S. president during his second term?

A. James Monroe.

Q. What house, built in Spotsylvania County about 1837 by John Lawrence Marye, utilized rejected Italian marble mantels originally intended for use in the White House?

A. Brompton.

Q. In what county was explorer William Clark born?

A. Caroline.

———◆———

Q. The former bookstore of Parson Mason Locke Weems, now the Weems-Botts Museum, is in what community?

A. Dumfries.

Q. What Virginia manufacturer is the largest cigarette producer in the nation?

A. Philip Morris.

Q. Prior to its incorporation in 1839, Wytheville had been known by what other two names?

A. Abbeville and Evansham.

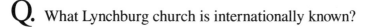

Q. Newspaperman Roger A. Pryor, who served as a foreign minister, congressman, and justice of the New York State Supreme Court, was born in what Virginia county?

A. Nottoway.

Q. What Lynchburg church is internationally known?

A. Thomas Road Baptist Church.

Q. What four towns have the shortest names in Virginia?

A. Ark, Dot, Ida, and Ivy.

Q. In what city did Confederate General J. E. B. Stuart die on May 12, 1864?

A. Richmond.

Q. Dinwiddie County was formed out of what county in 1752?

A. Prince George.

Q. What Virginia community contains Millionaires Row on Main Street?

A. Danville.

Q. Where was Zachary Taylor born on September 24, 1784?

A. Monte Bello House, near Barboursville.

Q. Under the promotion of General Fitzhugh Lee and his company, what town was founded in Rockbridge County in 1890?

A. Glasgow.

Q. King William County is the home of Indian reservations of which two tribes?

A. Pamunkey and Mattaponi.

Q. What parkway extends from the Shenandoah National Park in Virginia to the Great Smoky Mountains National Park of North Carolina and Tennessee?

A. The Blue Ridge Parkway.

Q. Confederate Secretary of War James Alexander Seddon was born in what Virginia town?

A. Falmouth.

Q. What two rivers run through Bath County, eventually joining to form the majestic James River?

A. Cowpasture and Jackson.

Q. Connelly's Tavern and Pigeon Run are former names of what Campbell County community?

A. Gladys.

Q. What is the name of the beautifully manicured yard in front of the Rotunda at the University of Virginia?

A. The Lawn.

Q. What is the name of the restored area of Richmond?

A. Fan District.

Q. Henrietta Hall, the first American woman missionary to China, was born in what Virginia town?

A. Kilmarnock.

Q. Who named Virginia the "Old Dominion"?

A. King Charles II.

Q. What were counties first called in Virginia?

A. Shires.

Q. The Grand Caverns in the upper Shenandoah Valley were once known by what name?

A. Weyer's Cave.

Q. General Alexander Leslie, along with his 3,000 troops, established a base at what Virginia city in October of 1780?

A. Portsmouth.

Q. Where did Virginia rank chronologically in acquiring statehood?

A. Tenth.

Q. What town is named for a favorite horse of Colonel James Rice?

A. Lawrenceville.

Q. Before it became the seat of government for Dickerson County in 1882, Clintwood was known by what name?

A. Holly Creek.

Q. What river forms the northeastern border of Virginia?

A. The Potomac River.

Q. In what town was the Eastern Shore Produce Exchange organized in 1899?

A. Onley.

Q. Who settled the northern community of Waterford, now a National Historic Landmark?

A. Quakers from Pennsylvania.

Q. Where is the Tomb of the Unknown Soldier of the Revolutionary War?

A. Old Presybterian Meeting House, Alexandria.

Q. The Masonic Lodge into which George Washington was initiated in 1752 still stands in what city?

A. Fredericksburg.

Q. Internationally known teacher and surgeon Dr. John Peter Mettauer was born in what Virginia community in 1787?

A. Kingsville.

Q. Marshall was first known by what name?

A. Salem.

Q. What county was named for the person acclaimed by England as the "conqueror of Canada"?

A. Amherst, for Sir Jeffrey Amherst.

Q. In 1753 John Cocke laid out the town of Guilford, which became what present-day Surry County community?

A. Cabin Point.

Q. Under the first charter of colonization in 1606, how far west did Virginia extend?

A. To the Pacific Ocean.

Q. In what town are Washington and Lee College and Virginia Military Institute?

A. Lexington.

Q. What tobacco plantation outside Charlottesville was built for James Monroe and his wife?

A. Ash Lawn, then called Highland.

Q. What present-day museum was the site of George Washington's last two birthday celebrations?

A. Gadsby's Tavern Museum, Alexandria.

Q. The Atlantic Command of what alliance is headquartered at the Norfolk Naval Base?

A. NATO.

Q. In whose home at Appomattox did generals Ulysses S. Grant and Robert E. Lee meet to draw up terms of surrender for the Confederacy?

A. The Wilmer McLean House.

Q. What is the world's largest bridge–tunnel complex?

A. The Chesapeake Bay Bridge–Tunnel.

Q. In what county was Nathaniel Bacon stricken with fever from which he died?

A. Gloucester.

Q. In what county was George Washington born?

A. Westmoreland.

Q. Pungoteague, which served as the seat of Accomac County between 1662 and 1677, has what Indian meaning?

A. "Place of fine sand."

Q. What was the name of the home and estate of Martha Dandridge Custis when she married George Washington in 1759?

A. The White House.

Q. General Grant, along with his staff, stayed at what Culpeper hotel in April of 1864?

A. The Virginia Hotel.

Q. For whom was Abb's Valley in Tazewell County named?

A. Absolom Looney.

Q. Where is the Virginia Military Institute?

A. Lexington.

Q. Richmond is the site of what gracious Tudor manor house originally built in fifteenth-century England?

A. Agecroft Hall.

Q. During his pre-military days, Winfield Scott maintained a law office in what town?

A. Dinwiddie.

Q. Where did Alice Scott Chandler establish The Home School in 1868?

A. Bowling Green.

Q. How many counties comprise the Commonwealth of Virginia?

A. Ninety-five.

Q. Where is the zero mile marker on the northeastern end of the Blue Ridge Parkway?

A. Rock Fish Gap.

Q. Due to feuds among early settlers, by what name was Max Meadows at one time called?

A. Valley of Contention and Strife.

Q. At what plantation near Hopewell may an eighteenth-century-style working windmill be viewed?

A. Flowerdew Hundred.

Q. The seven-mile stretch of U.S. 522 that runs south from Winchester and past the Shenandoah Memorial Park received what name in November of 1986?

A. Patsy Cline Memorial Highway.

Q. Bland County was formed in 1861 from parts of what three counties?

A. Giles, Tazewell, and Wythe.

Q. What Danville manufacturing business is the largest single-unit textile mill in the world?

A. Dan River, Inc.'s, Schoolfield plant.

Q. The majestic marble palace, Swannanoa, in the Shenandoah Valley, is near what community?

A. Waynesboro.

Q. Where is Patrick Henry buried?

A. Red Hill, Charlotte County.

Q. Charlottesville is the seat of what county?

A. Albemarle.

Q. Including its tributaries, what is the total drainage area of the Potomac River?

A. 5,960 square miles.

Q. Where did President Abraham Lincoln hold an informal peace meeting on February 2, 1865, with Confederate vice-president Stephens and Confederate commissioners?

A. Hampton Roads.

Q. Where were Lord Dunmore's troops routed by militia of the Committee of Safety on December 9, 1775?

A. Great Bridge.

Q. Founded in 1831, what Smyth County town was named for the famous "Swamp Fox" of South Carolina?

A. Marion, for Francis Marion.

Q. What change in the boundary of Virginia occurred on June 20, 1863?

A. West Virginia became a separate state.

Q. For whom was Newport News named?

A. Captain Christopher Newport, who brought news that more settlers were coming.

Q. The main supply of salt for the Confederacy came from what Virginia town?

A. Saltville.

Q. What is the seat of Loudoun County?

A. Leesburg.

Q. Near what town did Thomas Jefferson investigate an Indian burial mound and report on his findings in his *Notes on Virginia?*

A. Ruckersville.

Q. At what county courthouse did a shootout on March 12, 1912, leave the judge, an attorney, the sheriff, the jury foreman, and a witness for the prosecution dead?

A. Carroll County Courthouse, Hillsville.

Q. Historic Hollywood Cemetery is in what city?

A. Richmond.

Q. Thornburg was formerly called by what name?

A. Mud Tavern.

Q. Where is Paul D. Camp Community College?

A. Franklin.

Q. What lake is near the Booker T. Washington National Monument?

A. Smith Mountain Lake.

Q. Massanutten Caverns are near what community?

A. Keezletown, just east of Harrisonburg.

Q. Where is the James Madison Museum?

A. Orange.

Q. The first commercial canal in the United States opened in 1790 between what two Virginia cities?

A. Richmond and Westham.

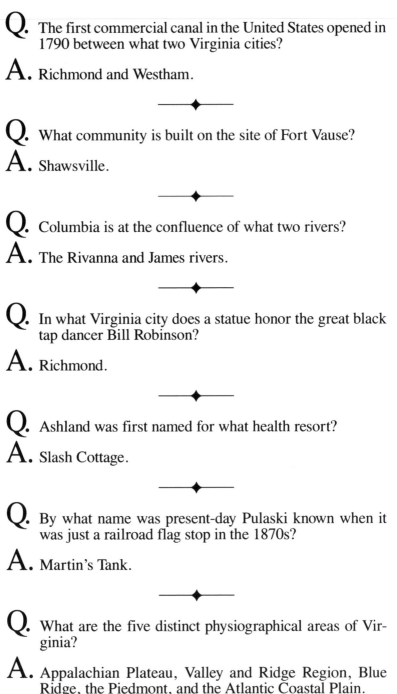

Q. What community is built on the site of Fort Vause?

A. Shawsville.

Q. Columbia is at the confluence of what two rivers?

A. The Rivanna and James rivers.

Q. In what Virginia city does a statue honor the great black tap dancer Bill Robinson?

A. Richmond.

Q. Ashland was first named for what health resort?

A. Slash Cottage.

Q. By what name was present-day Pulaski known when it was just a railroad flag stop in the 1870s?

A. Martin's Tank.

Q. What are the five distinct physiographical areas of Virginia?

A. Appalachian Plateau, Valley and Ridge Region, Blue Ridge, the Piedmont, and the Atlantic Coastal Plain.

Q. Where was Edith Bolling Wilson, wife of President Woodrow Wilson, born?

A. Wytheville.

Q. Residents of what community were prevented from constructing wooden chimneys and raising hogs by an act of the burgesses in 1748?

A. Walker Town, now Walkerton.

Q. What is unique about the Ball's Bluff National Cemetery in Loudoun County?

A. It is the smallest national cemetery in the nation.

Q. How many electoral votes are allocated to Virginia?

A. Thirteen.

Q. What Prince George County community developed around the E. I. du Pont de Nemours Company's munitions plant built in 1913?

A. Hopewell.

Q. Portions of Lee, Washington, and Russell counties were used to form what county?

A. Scott.

Q. St. Paul's College is in what town?

A. Lawrenceville.

Q. What town named for a mountain evergreen sits on the Carroll–Grayson County line?

A. Galax.

Q. What is the maximum north-to-south width of the state of Virginia?

A. 200 miles.

Q. Present-day Bristol was incorporated under what name in 1856?

A. Goodson.

Q. What northern county is known as "Hunt Country"?

A. Loudoun.

Q. Alexandria is on the west bank of what river?

A. The Potomac.

Q. Due to James Monroe's attempts at the repatriation of blacks to Africa, what Liberian city was named in his honor?

A. Monrovia.

Q. What is the Virginia state motto?

A. *Sic Semper Tyrannis* ("Thus always to tyrants").

Q. What city ranks second in population in Virginia?

A. Norfolk.

Q. Arlington National Cemetery surrounds whose home?

A. Robert E. Lee.

Q. What town became the official mail distribution center for southwest Virginia in 1793?

A. Abingdon.

Q. What city was the capital of the Confederacy, April 3–10, 1865?

A. Danville.

Q. How many victims of the War Between the States are buried at the Fredericksburg National Military Cemetery?

A. 15,206.

Q. What is the southwesternmost county in Virginia?

A. Lee County.

Q. What natural deepwater harbor forms Norfolk's northwestern boundary?

A. Hampton Roads.

Q. What is the total area of Virginia, excluding Chesapeake Bay?

A. 40,817 square miles.

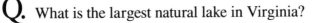

Q. Prior to 1882, Roanoke was known by what name?

A. Big Lick.

Q. The Virginia Manual Labor School was founded in what community by Dr. John H. Smythe in 1897?

A. Hanover.

Q. What is the largest natural lake in Virginia?

A. Lake Drummond, in Dismal Swamp.

Q. John Sevier, who became the governor of the State of Franklin and of Tennessee, owned land between 1761 and 1774 that became what town?

A. New Market.

Q. What Presbyterian church established at Abingdon in 1772 is called "the mother church of the Appalachies"?

A. Sinking Springs Church.

Q. Where was the longest battle of the War Between the States fought?

A. Near Petersburg.

Q. What is the highest elevation in Virginia?

A. 5,719 feet, Mount Rogers.

———◆———

Q. Before Lebanon became the county seat in 1816, what town served as the seat of Russell County?

A. Dickensonville.

———◆———

Q. What mansion was designated as a memorial to Robert E. Lee in 1955?

A. Arlington House.

———◆———

Q. Big Stone Gap was formerly called by what name?

A. Three Forks.

———◆———

Q. What is the name of the Virginia legislature?

A. The General Assembly.

———◆———

Q. Where may the marked church pews of George Washington and Robert E. Lee be seen?

A. Christ Church, Alexandria.

———◆———

Q. Smithfield Plantation, Blacksburg, was the birthplace of what two Virginia governors?

A. James Patton Preston and John Buchanan Floyd.

Q. Because Virginia has been the birthplace of so many U.S. presidents, what nickname has been given her?

A. "Mother of Presidents."

———◆———

Q. What town in Shenandoah County has previously been known as Shenandoah River, Funk's Mill, Funkstown, and Staufferstadt (Stovertown)?

A. Strasburg.

———◆———

Q. A bloody engagement between Cherokee and Shawnee warriors led to the naming of what Tazewell County peak?

A. Battle Knob.

———◆———

Q. Where does Virginia rank in population compared to the other states?

A. Twelfth.

———◆———

Q. In what Richmond building did Patrick Henry give his famous "Give me liberty or give me death" speech?

A. St. Johns Church.

———◆———

Q. At 5,520 feet, what is the second highest mountain in Virginia?

A. Whitetop.

———◆———

Q. The old towns of Belfield and Hicksford (or Hicksville) on either side of the Meherrin River combined to form what present-day town?

A. Emporia.

Q. What is the largest city in the Shenandoah Valley?

A. Roanoke.

Q. A fixed boundary between Maryland and what Virginia peninsula county was established in 1894?

A. Accomac.

Q. What Southampton County town was called Jerusalem until 1888?

A. Courtland.

Q. Virginia's "war governor," John Letcher, is buried in what graveyard?

A. Stonewall Jackson Memorial Cemetery.

Q. What international airport is in Loudoun County?

A. Dulles International Airport.

Q. Where does Norfolk Naval Base rank in size nationally?

A. First.

Q. What states border Virginia?

A. North Carolina, Tennessee, Kentucky, West Virginia, and Maryland.

Q. What municipality has the largest population in Virginia?

A. Virginia Beach.

———◆———

Q. In what community did hickory-rod coops for shipping chickens originate in 1885?

A. Brightwood.

———◆———

Q. Mary Baldwin College is in what city?

A. Staunton.

———◆———

Q. What is the highest court in Virginia?

A. The Supreme Court of Virginia.

———◆———

Q. The Mattaponi and Pamunkey rivers merge at West Point to form what river?

A. The York.

———◆———

Q. What town is named for the four West brothers, three of whom became governors of Virginia?

A. West Point.

———◆———

Q. Where did Lord Cornwallis surrender his troops on April 19, 1781?

A. Yorktown.

Q. Because of its limestone outcroppings, Harrisonburg was originally called by what name?

A. Rocktown.

Q. Where was General George C. Marshall buried in October, 1959?

A. Arlington National Cemetery.

Q. What unpopular name was first given to Gloucester?

A. Botetourt Town.

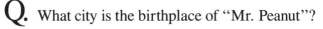

Q. In whose honor was "James Towne" (Jamestown) named?

A. King James I of England.

Q. What city is the birthplace of "Mr. Peanut"?

A. Suffolk.

Q. In what Alexandria house did the famous family, the Lees of Virginia, live?

A. Lee–Fendall House.

Q. Virginia is one of how many states designated as commonwealths?

A. Four.

Q. What town is the oldest incorporated community west of the Blue Ridge Mountains?

A. Abingdon.

Q. A statue of what man is under the dome of the Virginia State Capitol?

A. George Washington.

Q. What Virginia town, destroyed by fire in 1796, was reconstructed with funding from lottery proceeds?

A. Lexington.

Q. For whom was Orange County named?

A. The Dutch Prince of Orange, who became King William III of England.

Q. What is the seat of Pittsylvania County?

A. Chatham.

Q. Wise is the home of what college?

A. Clinch Valley College.

Q. What town was burned by Nathaniel Bacon and his men?

A. Jamestown.

Q. What Virginia community is known as the "City of Churches"?

A. Lynchburg.

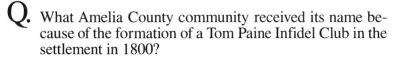

Q. What Amelia County community received its name because of the formation of a Tom Paine Infidel Club in the settlement in 1800?

A. Painesville.

Q. Mount Rogers is in what counties?

A. Grayson and Smyth counties.

Q. In what city was Rear Admiral Richard E. Byrd born?

A. Winchester.

Q. In what Colonial Heights house did General Robert E. Lee maintain his headquarters from June to September in 1864?

A. Violet Bank.

Q. On what river is Narrows situated?

A. New River.

Q. James Simpson laid out what Roanoke County town on sixteen acres of land in 1802?

A. Salem.

Q. Warrenton, seat of Fauquier County, is named for what hero of Bunker Hill?

A. General William Warren.

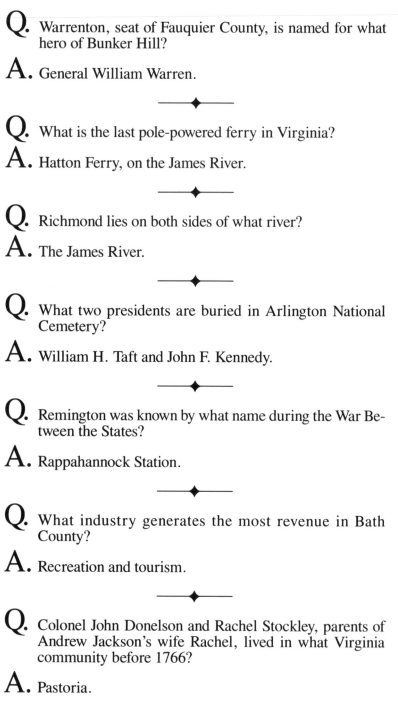

Q. What is the last pole-powered ferry in Virginia?

A. Hatton Ferry, on the James River.

Q. Richmond lies on both sides of what river?

A. The James River.

Q. What two presidents are buried in Arlington National Cemetery?

A. William H. Taft and John F. Kennedy.

Q. Remington was known by what name during the War Between the States?

A. Rappahannock Station.

Q. What industry generates the most revenue in Bath County?

A. Recreation and tourism.

Q. Colonel John Donelson and Rachel Stockley, parents of Andrew Jackson's wife Rachel, lived in what Virginia community before 1766?

A. Pastoria.

Q. What community was the birthplace of Booker T. Washington?

A. Hardy.

Q. Henry Alexander Wise, governor of Virginia from 1856 to 1860, was a native of what town?

A. Accomac.

Q. What Frederick County town was previously known as New Town?

A. Stephens City.

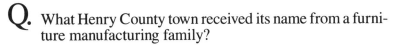

Q. Moccasin Gap is a pass on what mountain?

A. Clinch Mountain.

Q. What Henry County town received its name from a furniture manufacturing family?

A. Bassett.

Q. Blacksburg is in what county?

A. Montgomery.

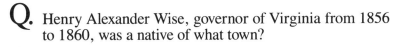

Q. What stream flows through Natural Tunnel in Scott County?

A. Stock Creek.

Q. What street in Bristol is the dividing line between Virginia and Tennessee?

A. State Street.

———◆———

Q. Hans Meadows, founded in 1792, is presently known by what name?

A. Christianburg.

———◆———

Q. In 1762 what town became the seat of Prince William County?

A. Dumfries.

———◆———

Q. Before being relocated in Farmville in 1871, where was the seat of Prince Edward County?

A. Worsham.

———◆———

Q. How did the community of Abingdon get its name?

A. It was named for the ancestral home of Martha Washington.

———◆———

Q. What is Virginia's largest geographical area?

A. The Piedmont.

———◆———

Q. Woodstock was given what name in 1761 in honor of Jacob Miller?

A. Müllerstadt.

Q. What is the largest employer in Norfolk?

A. The Norfolk Naval Base.

Q. In what county was Sam Houston born in 1793?

A. Rockbridge.

Q. From what county was Stafford County formed in 1664?

A. Westmoreland.

Q. What two Indian reservations are in King William County?

A. Mattaponi and Pamunkey Indian reservations.

Q. What location on the Potomac River was selected in 1917 for the establishment of a Marine Corps training facility?

A. Quantico.

Q. What large Confederate hospital at Richmond treated nearly 76,000 patients during the War Between the States?

A. Chimborazo General.

Q. What town in 1855 was named for Henry Clay's Kentucky estate?

A. Ashland.

Q. What town was the colonial capital of Virginia?

A. Williamsburg.

———◆———

Q. In what city is the oldest existing fire house in Virginia?

A. Richmond, Steamer Company Number 5.

———◆———

Q. What city was founded at the crossroads of Spotswood Trail and Indian Road in 1780?

A. Harrisonburg.

———◆———

Q. What large county in the Shenandoah Valley was settled by Scotch-Irish immigrants and is still considered a Scotch-Irish community?

A. Augusta.

———◆———

Q. What is the maximum east-to-west length of Virginia?

A. 432 miles.

———◆———

Q. By what other name do geographers refer to the Appalachian Plateau?

A. The Southwestern Plateau.

———◆———

Q. From what town did the locomotive, the "Old 97," set forth in 1903 on its final run, according to the well-known ballad?

A. Monroe.

ENTERTAINMENT

C H A P T E R   T W O

Q. The famous Statler Brothers hail from what Virginia city?

A. Staunton.

Q. In 1984 what Virginia-born actor created for television a memorable Scrooge in Charles Dickens's *A Christmas Carol?*

A. George C. Scott.

Q. By what nickname was the great tap dancer Bill Robinson known?

A. "Bojangles."

Q. Chicken Pluckers Fun Day is part of what Harrisonburg celebration?

A. Virginia Poultry Festival.

Q. In 1946 what Newport News-born singer/actress made her stage debut in *St. Louis Woman?*

A. Pearl Bailey.

Q. What Portsmouth-born saxophonist and flautist became the first musician to record jazz flute solos?

A. Wayman Carver.

Q. Shirley Temple starred with what Virginia-born actor in *Rebecca of Sunnybrook Farm?*

A. Randolph Scott.

Q. The White Water Canyon rafting ride may be enjoyed at what Virginia theme park?

A. Kings Dominion.

Q. What newly revamped Portsmouth waterfront offers restaurants, shopping, and live entertainment?

A. Portside.

Q. Where was Ella Fitzgerald born in 1918?

A. Newport News.

Q. What Virginia-born lyricist wrote the hit song "Chapel of Love" recorded by the Dixie Cups?

A. George Morton.

Q. The Carter Family made their first commercial recording in what year?

A. 1927.

Q. What Virginia-born comedian appeared on such television shows as "That's My Mama," "WKRP in Cincinnati," and "Simon and Simon"?

A. Tim Reid.

Q. What southwest Virginia theater served as a learning ground for such greats as Gregory Peck, Patricia Neal, and Ernest Borgnine?

A. The Barter Theatre.

Q. Alan Alda and Carol Burnett starred in what 1981 movie filmed in part in Virginia?

A. *The Four Seasons.*

Q. What Lynchburg-born performer was named Most Promising Male Country Artist of 1966 by *Billboard Magazine?*

A. Ray Pillow.

Q. Where is the Virginia Junior Miss Pageant held?

A. Fairfax.

Q. Trombonist Albert Thornton ("Al") Grey, who became internationally known while working with the Count Basie orchestra from 1957 through 1961, was born in what Virginia town?

A. Aldie.

Q. Mountain Lake Hotel in Giles County was featured in what movie starring Patrick Swayze and Jennifer Grey?

A. *Dirty Dancing.*

Q. What event ushers in the celebration of Christmas at Williamsburg?

A. The Grand Illumination.

Q. Bluegrass great Mac Wiseman was born in what Shenandoah Valley community?

A. Crimora.

Q. In 1962, Ella Fitzgerald received what award for the album *Ella Swings Brightly with Nelson Riddle?*

A. A Grammy Award for Best Female Vocalist.

Q. Fireworks, roaring cannons, and a Pirate's Ball are all a part of what May Festival in Norfolk?

A. Harborfest.

Q. What character did Freeman Gosden play on the highly successful "Amos 'n Andy" radio show?

A. Amos Jones, the taxicab driver.

Q. The Lucketts County Fair is held in what town?
A. Leesburg.

Q. Songwriter George ("Shadow") Morton was born in what city?

A. Richmond.

Q. The Oscar for what 1970 Best Motion Picture of the Year is displayed at the George C. Marshall Museum in Lexington?

A. *Patton.*

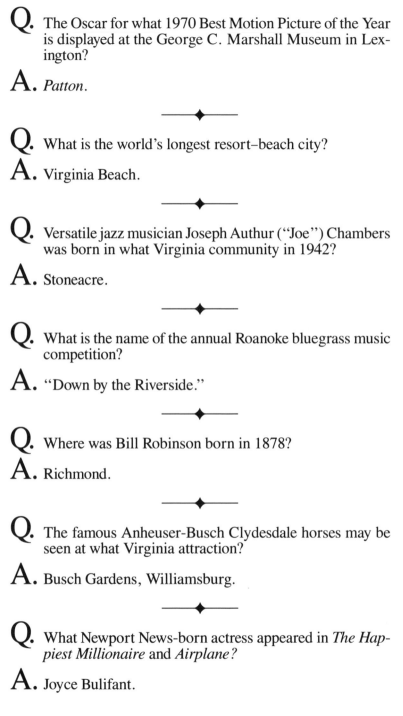

Q. What is the world's longest resort–beach city?

A. Virginia Beach.

Q. Versatile jazz musician Joseph Authur ("Joe") Chambers was born in what Virginia community in 1942?

A. Stoneacre.

Q. What is the name of the annual Roanoke bluegrass music competition?

A. "Down by the Riverside."

Q. Where was Bill Robinson born in 1878?

A. Richmond.

Q. The famous Anheuser-Busch Clydesdale horses may be seen at what Virginia attraction?

A. Busch Gardens, Williamsburg.

Q. What Newport News-born actress appeared in *The Happiest Millionaire* and *Airplane?*

A. Joyce Bulifant.

Q. Actor Joseph Cotten was born May 15, 1905, in what Virginia city?

A. Petersburg.

———◆———

Q. What 1984 Warner Brothers movie starring Goldie Hawn was filmed in Virginia?

A. *Protocol.*

———◆———

Q. Bealeton is the home of what entertaining aeronautical show?

A. The Flying Circus.

———◆———

Q. On what television series did Richmond-born Mac-Kenzie Phillips co-star with Valerie Bertinelli?

A. "One Day at a Time."

———◆———

Q. The Mountain Magic in May Festival may be enjoyed in what community?

A. Buchanan.

———◆———

Q. What was Mac Wiseman's first major hit recording for Dot Records?

A. " 'Tis Sweet to Be Remembered."

———◆———

Q. What Virginia town acquired the first licensed Elvis Presley Museum outside of Graceland?

A. Dale City.

Q. What television series was built around the family stories of Earl Hamner, Jr.?

A. "The Waltons."

Q. The Northern Shenandoah Valley provides a step into the prehistoric world of mammoths and cave men at what attraction?

A. Dinosaur Land.

Q. Kylene Baker of Galax received what coveted award in 1979?

A. Miss America.

Q. What was Bill Robinson's real name?

A. Luther Robinson.

Q. Drummer Wilmore ("Slick") Jones, who was a sideman with Fletcher Henderson and Fats Waller, was born in what Virginia city?

A. Roanoke.

Q. Which is the only national park in the nation devoted to the performing arts?

A. Wolf Trap Farm Park.

Q. At what Staunton location do the Statler Brothers present their annual Fourth of July concert?

A. Gypsy Hill Park.

Q. What was Wayne Newton's first hit single, which was produced by his friend, Bobby Darin?

A. "Danke Schoen."

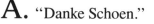

Q. Where was Warren Beatty born on March 30, 1938?

A. Richmond.

Q. What 1959 recording by Portsmouth teenager Tommy ("Bubba") Facenda was made in twenty-eight different versions?

A. "High School U.S.A."

Q. Clifford is host to what activity in the fall?

A. The Sorghum Molasses Festival.

Q. Where can one enjoy watching wing walking, precision aerobatics, hot-air ballooning, skydiving, and comedy?

A. Flying Circus Aerodrome near Bealeton.

Q. Where is the Southside Tobacco Farmers' BBQ Festival held?

A. Chase City.

Q. What country music showplace in Mathews County is known as "Virginia's Little Ole Opry"?

A. Donk's.

Q. Tim Reid played what character on the television series "WKRP in Cincinnati"?

A. Venus Flytrap.

Q. Urbana celebrates what annual two-day event the first weekend in November?

A. The Oyster Festival.

Q. The Portside amphitheater features what unusual entertainment structure?

A. A floating stage.

Q. What movie filmed in part in Virginia is based on the life of country music star Loretta Lynn?

A. *Coal Miner's Daughter*.

Q. Where is the nation's oldest and largest fiddlers' convention held each August?

A. Galax.

Q. For what movie was the Jefferson Hotel in Richmond the setting?

A. *My Dinner with André*.

Q. Fresh cider, apple butter, and apple picking are all part of what fall event in Syria?

A. Apple Harvest Festival.

Q. Versatile country/pop singer Juice Newton was born in what seaside Virginia community?

A. Virginia Beach.

◆

Q. What 1980 CBS Movie of the Week starring Jason Miller, Christine Lahti, Stephen Collins, and David Spielberg was filmed in part in Virginia?

A. *The Henderson Monster*.

◆

Q. What Portsmouth-born drummer and music educator took time off from his musical career to fly a private jet for lawyer F. Lee Bailey?

A. Samuel David ("Dave") Bailey.

◆

Q. Virginia-born Roy Clark came into national prominence on what television show?

A. "Hee-Haw."

◆

Q. "Mama, He Treats Your Daughter Mean" was an early 1950s rhythm and blues hit by what Portsmouth-born singer?

A. Ruth Brown.

◆

Q. The family entertainment park Kings Dominion is in what community?

A. Doswell.

◆

Q. In what movie did Richmond-born actress Shirley Mac-Laine make her screen debut in 1955?

A. *The Trouble with Harry*.

Q. Where was movie director Henry King born?

A. Christianburg.

Q. The Pork, Peanut, and Pine Festival is a July event held in what community?

A. Surry.

Q. "Radio's Own Statue of Liberty," Kate Smith, was born in what Virginia city?

A. Greenville.

Q. Norfolk offers entertainment and shopping at what festival marketplace?

A. The Waterside.

Q. What Virginia-born actor appeared in such movies as *Tin Pan Alley, Footlight Serenade*, and *Sentimental Journey?*

A. John Payne.

Q. Where was record producer Creed Taylor born in 1929?

A. Lynchburg.

———◆———

Q. What Virginia Military Institute graduate produced the movie *Patton?*

A. General Frank McCarthy.

Q. Lexington offers summer stock at what historic downtown facility?

A. The Henry Street Playhouse.

◆

Q. George Morton wrote what number one hit in 1964 that was recorded by the Shangri-Las?

A. "Leader of the Pack."

◆

Q. The nation's largest parade to celebrate George Washington's birthday is held in what Virginia city?

A. Alexandria.

◆

Q. Where was June Carter born on June 23, 1929?

A. Maces Springs.

◆

Q. Where is the World Tobacco Auctioneering Championship held?

A. Danville.

◆

Q. What city has a popular Scottish Christmas walk every December?

A. Alexandria.

◆

Q. The zest of a colonial fair is recreated during what September celebration at Williamsburg?

A. Publick Times and Fair Days.

Q. A zoological park, science museum, botanical garden, aquarium, and planatarium are combined into what single complex in Newport News?

A. Virginia Living Museum.

Q. Where is Nostalgiafest held?

A. Petersburg.

Q. Richmond Crinkley, who produced the Tony award-winning *Elephant Man,* was born in what Virginia town?

A. Blackstone.

Q. Veteran movie actor John Payne made his 1973 stage debut in what theatrical production?

A. *Good News*.

Q. What roller coaster ride at Busch Gardens makes use of 360-degree loops?

A. The Loch Ness Monster.

Q. Tazewell is the birthplace of what television and movie actress?

A. Kathryn Harrold.

Q. The Fairfax County Fair is held each Father's Day weekend on what college campus?

A. George Mason University.

Q. A waiters' race and wine tasting are a sampling of what Middleburg celebration?

A. The annual Wine Festival.

Q. What was Shirley MacLaine's original name?

A. Shirley Beatty.

Q. What Virginia-born actress appeared in the television production "The Grass Is Always Greener over the Septic Tank"?

A. Lauri Hendler.

Q. In what Virginia county was Randolph Scott born?

A. Orange.

Q. Who is the only person with a mother, uncle, aunt, and husband in the Country Music Hall of Fame?

A. June Carter.

Q. What banjo virtuoso, born in Dooley, became famous in the 1950s and 1960s with his two-finger, one-thumb-style of playing?

A. Moran L. ("Dock") Boggs.

Q. Virginia-born Kate Smith appeared with what other famous American in the 1943 movie *This Is the Army?*

A. Ronald Reagan.

Q. What Richmond-born television staff musician played on such shows as the "Carol Burnett Show," "Flip Wilson Show," and "Sammy Davis Show."

A. George ("Red") Callender.

Q. Legend says that the staircase in what movie was modeled after the one in the Jefferson Hotel in Richmond?

A. *Gone With The Wind.*

Q. Thomas Jefferson's Tomatoe Faire is hosted by what city?

A. Lynchburg.

Q. What is western Virginia's largest fair?

A. Roanoke's Country Livin' Festival.

Q. In what city was Freeman Gosden, the co-star of the famous "Amos 'n Andy" radio show, born in 1899?

A. Richmond.

Q. Theatrical portrayals of ghosts, myths, and legends are the focal point of what Portsmouth Halloween event?

A. Olde Towne Ghost Walk.

Q. What Norfolk-born singer appeared in the movie *Thunder Road?*

A. Keely Smith.

Q. Longtime "Tonight Show" musician Tommy Newsom was born in what Virginia city?

A. Portsmouth.

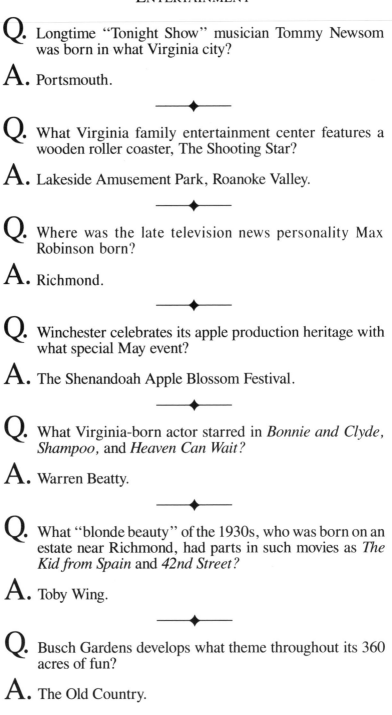

Q. What Virginia family entertainment center features a wooden roller coaster, The Shooting Star?

A. Lakeside Amusement Park, Roanoke Valley.

Q. Where was the late television news personality Max Robinson born?

A. Richmond.

Q. Winchester celebrates its apple production heritage with what special May event?

A. The Shenandoah Apple Blossom Festival.

Q. What Virginia-born actor starred in *Bonnie and Clyde*, *Shampoo*, and *Heaven Can Wait?*

A. Warren Beatty.

Q. What "blonde beauty" of the 1930s, who was born on an estate near Richmond, had parts in such movies as *The Kid from Spain* and *42nd Street?*

A. Toby Wing.

Q. Busch Gardens develops what theme throughout its 360 acres of fun?

A. The Old Country.

Q. What Virginia senator was married to Elizabeth Taylor?

A. John Warner.

Q. Where was entertainer Wayne Newton born on April 3, 1942?

A. Norfolk.

Q. What September event in Edinburg features pork skin frying, quilting, and broom making?

A. The Edinburg Ole Time Festival.

Q. Grand Ole Opry star Ray Pillow starred in what 1960s movie?

A. *Country Boy.*

Q. What Richmond-born personality was co-host on the television show "That's Incredible"?

A. Fran Tarkenton.

Q. What song, co-written and recorded by Gene Vincent and the Bluecaps in 1956, became number seven nationwide?

A. "Be-Bop-a-Lula."

Q. What 1984 movie built around an old-fashioned rural drama, starring Mel Gibson and Sissy Spacek, was filmed in Virginia?

A. *The River.*

Q. What Portsmouth-born singer/songwriter/producer became known as "Swamp Dogg"?

A. Jerry Williams.

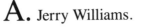

Q. Lynchburg-born actor Carl Anderson played what role in the film *Jesus Christ Superstar?*

A. Judas.

Q. Warsaw is the site of what fun-filled event in the fall?

A. Oktoberfest.

Q. What 1980 science fiction movie starring Kirk Douglas, Martin Sheen, and Katherine Ross was shot in part in Virginia?

A. *The Final Countdown.*

Q. What seashore celebration is held each September at Virginia Beach?

A. The Virginia Beach Neptune Festival.

Q. George C. Scott starred in what CBS television series?

A. "East Side, West Side."

Q. "Hey There, Lonely Girl" was a number two hit in 1970 by what Norfolk-born rhythm and blues artist?

A. Eddie Holman.

Q. Where was the legendary country singing star Patsy Cline born?

A. Winchester.

Q. Joseph Cotten made his film debut in what 1941 motion picture?

A. *Citizen Kane*.

Q. With what great orchestra did Roy Clark perform during the summer of 1976?

A. Arthur Fiedler and the Boston Pops Orchestra.

Q. The Oh Shenandoah pageant is part of what October festivities in Luray?

A. Page County Heritage Festival.

Q. What book and movie brought Chincoteague to national attention?

A. *Misty of Chincoteague*.

Q. What was the Carter family's biggest hit, recorded in 1928?

A. "Wildwood Flower."

Q. Lexington is the site of what annual birthday party on January 21?

A. Stonewall Jackson's Birthday Celebration.

Q. Actress Lynn Bari, who was born in Roanoke, made her first screen appearance in what movie?

A. *Dancing Lady.*

Q. In what Virginia city was versatile guitarist and composer Charles L. ("Charlie") Byrd born in 1925?

A. Suffolk.

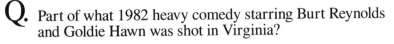

Q. Where was rockabilly singer Gene Vincent born?

A. Norfolk.

Q. Oinks of delight and squeals of fun are all a part of what June event in Emporia?

A. The Virginia Pork Festival.

Q. Part of what 1982 heavy comedy starring Burt Reynolds and Goldie Hawn was shot in Virginia?

A. *Best Friends.*

Q. What city is home to the Miss Virginia Pageant?

A. Roanoke.

Q. For what motion picture did Warren Beatty receive an Academy Award as Best Director?

A. *Reds.*

Q. What is the name of Lexington's outdoor theater which produces original works like *Stonewall Country*?

A. Lime Kiln Arts Theater at the Kiln.

Q. What water theme park now adds to the enjoyment of a stay at Virginia Beach?

A. Wild Water Rapids.

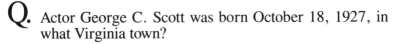

Q. In the film *The Higher We Fly*, Virginia Beach pilot Ken Kellett doubled for what performer?

A. John Denver.

Q. What family fun event is held annually at Falls Church?

A. The Great Falls Festival.

———◆———

Q. Actor George C. Scott was born October 18, 1927, in what Virginia town?

A. Wise.

———◆———

Q. What Coeburn-born brothers formed a bluegrass duo featuring the sounds of a mandolin?

A. Jim and Jesse McReynolds.

———◆———

Q. Where is the Tazewell County Fair and Festival held each year?

A. Richlands.

Q. Where in Virginia may a canine parade, a dog auction, and contests for the best-dressed, most humorous and ugliest dogs be enjoyed?

A. Dog Mart festivities at Fredericksburg.

Q. The Statler Brothers Museum is in what Staunton building?

A. The elementary school that they attended.

Q. What Berryville-born producer made such movies as *The Balcony*, *Lord of the Flies*, and *Fahrenheit 451*?

A. Lewis M. Allen.

Q. Gene Pitney's 1968 hit "She's a Heartbreaker" was written by what Virginia-born lyricist?

A. Swamp Dogg.

———————◆———————

Q. Country music entertainer Roy Clark was born in what Virginia community?

A. Meherrin.

———————◆———————

Q. What is actress Lynn Bari's real name?

A. Marjorie Bitzer.

———————◆———————

Q. Where is the Historic Farmers Market Festival held?

A. Richmond.

Q. What folk/country music legend was born on May 10, 1901, at Nickelsville in southwestern Virginia?

A. Mother Maybelle Carter.

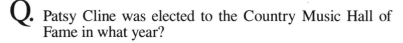

Q. Where is the Tri-State Gospel Singing held each September?

A. Breaks Interstate Park.

Q. Patsy Cline was elected to the Country Music Hall of Fame in what year?

A. 1973.

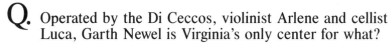

Q. In what Virginia city was actor John Payne born?

A. Roanoke.

Q. Operated by the Di Ceccos, violinist Arlene and cellist Luca, Garth Newel is Virginia's only center for what?

A. Studying and performing chamber music.

Q. What city is the site of the Kaleidoscope Festival?

A. Lynchburg.

Q. Actor/producer David Huddleston, who has been involved in such movies as *Rio Lobo, Blazing Saddles,* and *McQ,* is a native of what Virginia community?

A. Vinton.

Q. Virginian actress MacKenzie Phillips made her screen debut in 1973 in what movie?

A. *American Graffiti.*

———◆———

Q. What performer of stage and television was born in Fort Lee in 1948?

A. Victoria Mallory.

———◆———

Q. Kate Smith popularized what song, which became known as the nation's "second national anthem"?

A. "God Bless America."

———◆———

Q. The Double Rampage showers thrills of excitement in what multi-million-dollar Virginia water park?

A. Water Country USA, Williamsburg.

———◆———

Q. Older, traditional craftsmen and musicians pass on their talents at what Ferrum College mountain music event?

A. The Folk Life Festival.

———◆———

Q. What is the name of the public playground near the Virginia Beach–Norfolk Expressway that features skateboard bowls and soapbox derby ramps?

A. Mount Trashmore.

———◆———

Q. Where was country music performer Joe Maphis born on May 12, 1921?

A. Suffolk.

HISTORY

C H A P T E R   T H R E E

Q. What Virginian is known as the "Father of the Constitution"?

A. James Madison.

Q. What notorious outlaw of the Cumberlands was hanged in 1892 at the Wise County Courthouse?

A. Talt Hall.

Q. What were the names of the three ships that landed the first colonists at Jamestown?

A. *Discovery, Godspeed,* and *Susan Constant.*

Q. In 1970 who became the first Republican to be elected governor in almost 100 years?

A. A. Linwood Holton, Jr.

Q. What assassin was cornered and fatally wounded by Federal troops on the Garrett farm near Port Royal on April 26, 1865?

A. John Wilkes Booth.

Q. What official response did the Virginia General Assembly pass on May 30, 1765, in response to the Stamp Act?

A. The Virginia Resolves.

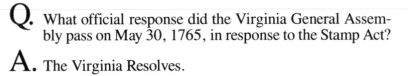

Q. Who laid out the 1816 Manchester and Petersburg Turnpike?

A. Claude Crozet.

Q. What two famous ironclads battled near Hampton Roads on March 9, 1862?

A. *Monitor* and *Merrimac*.

Q. The house where Woodrow Wilson was born was originally built for what purpose?

A. As a manse for Presbyterian ministers.

Q. What man was given the title "Voice of the Revolution"?

A. Patrick Henry.

Q. How many Virginia colonists were killed in a Powhatan Indian raid on March 22, 1622?

A. 347 (18 more died later of wounds).

Q. Virginia cast its electoral votes for what presidential candidate in 1988?

A. President George Bush.

Q. On what date did Virginia join the Confederate States of America?

A. May 21, 1861.

Q. What Virginian penned the Declaration of Independence?

A. Thomas Jefferson.

Q. What Virginia institution, founded in 1693, is the second oldest college in the United States?

A. The College of William and Mary.

Q. What faculty member at the Virginia Military Institute designed the armor for the Confederate ironclad *Merrimac*?

A. John Mercer Brooke.

Q. Among the original thirteen states, in what order did Virginia rank in the ratification of the Constitution?

A. Tenth.

Q. What Union army major general, born in Southampton County on July 31, 1816, was called the "Rock of Chickamauga"?

A. George H. Thomas.

Q. The Virginia Convention, acting as a legislative body, approved what document on June 12, 1776?

A. George Mason's Virginia Declaration of Rights.

Q. What was the name of General Stonewall Jackson's war horse?

A. Little Sorrel.

———◆———

Q. In an attempt to break through defenses around Richmond on July 30, 1864, how many pounds of gunpowder were detonated in a tunnel beneath Confederate lines by Federal forces?

A. 8,000.

———◆———

Q. What Hanover County resident was allowed to fire the first shot on Fort Sumter, beginning the War Between the States?

A. Edmund Ruffin.

———◆———

Q. Who was the first commander-in-chief of the Virginia forces?

A. Patrick Henry.

———◆———

Q. What document, famous for being the forerunner to the Declaration of Independence, was written at Lead Mines, now Austinville?

A. Fincastle Resolutions.

———◆———

Q. To what office was Thomas Jefferson appointed in July, 1789?

A. U.S. Secretary of State.

———◆———

Q. What Staunton building served as the state capitol during the Revolutionary War?

A. Trinity Church.

Q. Patrick Henry had how many children?

A. Seventeen.

———◆———

Q. What black free man of Richmond was hanged in 1800 on conspiracy charges to incite a black rebellion?

A. Gabriel Prosser.

———◆———

Q. What attorney general, who served under both James Monroe and John Quincy Adams, practiced law at Madison?

A. William Wirt.

———◆———

Q. With what 1804 acquisition did President Thomas Jefferson exceed his constitutional authority?

A. The Louisiana Purchase.

———◆———

Q. What black candidate for state senator was shot to death in Charlotte County in 1892?

A. John R. Holmes.

———◆———

Q. Sully Plantation was the home of what statesman, who was northern Virginia's first representative to Congress?

A. Richard Bland Lee.

———◆———

Q. In 1918, what two institutions became the first state-supported colleges to admit women?

A. Virginia Polytechnic Institute and the College of William and Mary.

Q. What battle on March 23, 1862, marked the beginning of General Thomas J. Jackson's valley campaign?

A. The Battle of Kernstown.

Q. How many turnpike companies were incorporated in Virginia between 1802 and 1818?

A. Eight.

Q. What institution of higher education for women opened at Staunton in 1842?

A. The Augusta Female Seminary, later called the Mary Baldwin Seminary.

Q. Dismissed burgesses drew up and adopted what agreement at Raleigh Tavern in Williamsburg in 1769?

A. The Non-importation Agreement.

Q. What heroine rode over forty miles through the mountains to save Wytheville from Union attack in July 1863?

A. Molly Tynes.

Q. When the first road surveyors were appointed in 1658, what was the width of the road right-of-way they were to maintain?

A. Forty feet.

Q. What important pronouncement of foreign policy was formulated during the administration of James Monroe?

A. The Monroe Doctrine.

Q. Who led Virginia's first rebellion against autocratic rule?

A. Nathaniel Bacon.

———◆———

Q. For thirty years the Robert E. Lees lived in what Virginia home?

A. Arlington House.

———◆———

Q. What was the first college for blacks in Virginia?

A. Virginia Normal and Collegiate Institute.

———◆———

Q. The Chesapeake Bay Bridge–Tunnel took how long to build?

A. Three years and six months.

———◆———

Q. What octagonal dwelling did Thomas Jefferson build as his personal retreat?

A. Poplar Forest, Bedford County.

———◆———

Q. What Byrd family home is considered to be one of the outstanding examples of Georgian architecture of Colonial times?

A. Westover.

———◆———

Q. What two amendments to the Constitution were ratified by Virginia on October 8, 1869?

A. The Fourteenth and Fifteenth amendments.

Q. Who did John Rolfe marry in 1614?

A. Pocahontas.

———◆———

Q. What was the status of the first twenty blacks to arrive in Virginia?

A. Indentured servants.

———◆———

Q. Work laws enacted by Virginia in 1889 established protective guidelines for what two sections of the labor force?

A. Women and children.

———◆———

Q. What nickname did runaway slave Henry Brown of Richmond receive in 1856 after arriving safely in Philadelphia in a crate measuring two feet, eight inches by two feet, three inches?

A. "Box Brown."

———◆———

Q. Who is buried in a marked grave outside Robert E. Lee's office in Lexington?

A. Traveller, Lee's beloved horse.

———◆———

Q. What was the first steam railroad to operate in Virginia?

A. The Petersburg Railroad Company.

———◆———

Q. What renowned World War II general spent his first year at Virginia Military Institute before transferring to West Point?

A. George S. Patton.

Q. Who was both the first free black and the first black land-owner in Virginia?

A. Anthony Johnson.

Q. What did George Mason name his beautiful plantation on the Potomac River?

A. Gunston Hall.

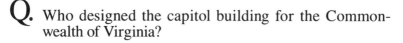

Q. Of the ten initial constitutional amendments that make up the Bill of Rights, how many were introduced by James Madison?

A. Nine.

Q. What state-fostered railroad was chartered in 1849?

A. The Blue Ridge Railroad Company.

Q. Who designed the capitol building for the Common-wealth of Virginia?

A. Thomas Jefferson.

Q. What is the oldest Methodist college in the United States?

A. Randolph-Macon.

Q. What ex-slave, born April 5, 1856, in Franklin County, became president and founder of Tuskegee Institute in Alabama?

A. Booker T. Washington.

Q. What church in Richmond was attended by Jefferson Davis and many members of his cabinet?

A. Old St. Paul's Episcopal, which honors Davis and his family with memorial plaques.

———◆———

Q. What highly respected Confederate general taught artillery tactics and natural philosophy at the Virginia Military Institute in the mid-1800s?

A. Stonewall Jackson.

———◆———

Q. In 1756 who discovered lead in the area now known as Austinville?

A. Colonel Chiswell.

———◆———

Q. How many black fraternal insurance companies were operating in Virginia in 1890?

A. About 200.

———◆———

Q. What mechanical agricultural implement did Cyrus McCormick develop in 1834?

A. The reaping machine.

———◆———

Q. After the death of Thomas Jefferson, who became rector (president) of the University of Virginia?

A. James Madison.

———◆———

Q. How many newspapers were there in Virginia in 1896?

A. 160.

Q. Who was placed in command of Virginia's troops on April 17, 1861?

A. Robert E. Lee.

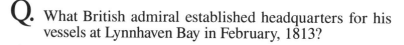

Q. What British admiral established headquarters for his vessels at Lynnhaven Bay in February, 1813?

A. Admiral George Cockburn.

Q. The Bill of Rights of the U.S. Constitution derived from what Virginia document?

A. The Virginia Declaration of Rights.

Q. For what purpose was the Virginia Military Institute originally established?

A. To guard the arsenal of the commonwealth.

Q. What male-only college was founded in 1776?

A. Hampden-Sydney.

Q. Danville is the birthplace of what lady who became the first woman to sit in the British House of Commons?

A. Lady Astor.

Q. What company sponsored the first colonists in Jamestown?

A. The Virginia Company of London.

Q. What eighteenth-century estate was the home of George and Martha Washington?

A. Mount Vernon.

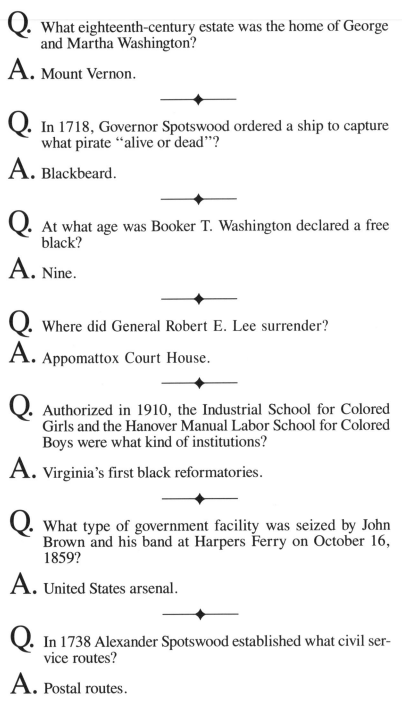

Q. In 1718, Governor Spotswood ordered a ship to capture what pirate "alive or dead"?

A. Blackbeard.

Q. At what age was Booker T. Washington declared a free black?

A. Nine.

Q. Where did General Robert E. Lee surrender?

A. Appomattox Court House.

Q. Authorized in 1910, the Industrial School for Colored Girls and the Hanover Manual Labor School for Colored Boys were what kind of institutions?

A. Virginia's first black reformatories.

Q. What type of government facility was seized by John Brown and his band at Harpers Ferry on October 16, 1859?

A. United States arsenal.

Q. In 1738 Alexander Spotswood established what civil service routes?

A. Postal routes.

Q. Where was Jefferson Davis when he received word that Richmond would have to be evacuated during the Civil War?

A. Saint Paul's Church, Richmond.

———◆———

Q. Who wrote George Washington's funeral oration, including the famous phrase "First in war, first in peace, and first in the hearts of his countrymen"?

A. "Light Horse" Harry Lee.

———◆———

Q. What document did Virginia ratify on June 26, 1786?

A. The Constitution of the United States.

———◆———

Q. Virginia's first Jewish congregation was established in what city in 1789?

A. Richmond.

———◆———

Q. On what date did George Washington take office as the first president of the United States?

A. April 30, 1789.

———◆———

Q. In what Danville home were the last meetings between President Jefferson Davis and his cabinet held?

A. The Sutherlin Mansion.

———◆———

Q. How many women were sent to the Virginia Colony in 1621 to become wives of settlers?

A. 150.

Q. In colonial times what type of large rolling containers, pulled by oxen or horses, were used to move tobacco overland?

A. Hogsheads.

———◆———

Q. In what city was Jefferson Davis arraigned and indicted for treason on May 13, 1867?

A. Richmond.

———◆———

Q. What two Virginians were outstanding heroes of the Mexican War?

A. Winfield Scott and Zachary Taylor.

———◆———

Q. What Virginian is known as the "great chief justice"?

A. John Marshall.

———◆———

Q. In reaction to the Boston Port Bill, the Virginia assembly attempted to set aside June 1, 1774, for what two activities?

A. Prayer and fasting.

———◆———

Q. On September 23, 1890, who became Virginia's first black representative in Congress?

A. John Mercer Langston.

———◆———

Q. An 1861 inventory of the estate of James Burroughs placed what value on one Negro boy, "Booker," who became the great black educator Booker T. Washington?

A. Four hundred dollars.

Q. At its completion in 1928, what bridge was billed as the longest all-over-water bridge in the world?

A. The Newport News–James River Bridge.

Q. Rebecca, Isaacke, and Elias Legardo, along with Joseph Moise, became the first persons of what ethnic group to enter Virginia in 1624?

A. Jews.

Q. Where are presidents James Monroe and John Tyler buried?

A. Hollywood Cemetery, Richmond.

Q. What labor group held its national convention at Richmond in 1886?

A. The Knights of Labor.

Q. The first official Thanksgiving in 1619 took place at what Virginia plantation?

A. Berkeley, Charles City County.

Q. What firm was Virginia's first cigarette manufacturer?

A. Allen & Ginter of Richmond.

Q. How many terms did James Monroe serve as president of the United States?

A. Two.

Q. What rebellion was launched by Virginia planters in 1682?

A. The Tobacco Riots.

Q. Who was elected Virginia's sixty-sixth governor?

A. L. Douglas Wilder.

Q. In what county was the first iron furnace in America established in 1619?

A. Chesterfield.

Q. What aviation record was set by Virginian adventurer Rear Admiral Richard E. Byrd on May 9, 1926?

A. He, along with co-pilot Floyd Bennett, were the first men to fly to the North Pole.

Q. In what Alexandria house did General Braddock meet with five colonial governors to execute early planning of the French and Indian War?

A. Carlyle House.

Q. The Virginia assembly passed what act in 1758?

A. The Two Penny Act.

Q. What type of con game was worked on the citizens of Waynesboro about 1895?

A. An oil hoax.

Q. What Clarke County-born bride became Mrs. Robert E. Lee on June 30, 1831?

A. Mary Anna Randolph Custis.

Q. How long was William Henry Harrison's tenure as president of the United States?

A. One month, March 4 to April 4, 1841.

Q. Who became governor of Virginia in the fall of 1768?

A. Lord Botetourt.

Q. What United States president held more major political offices than any other?

A. James Monroe: U.S. Senator, Minister to England, Minister to Spain, Minister to France, Governor of Virginia, Secretary of State, Secretary of War, and President of the United States.

Q. Virginia was the only southern state to support which Presidential candidate in 1976?

A. Gerald Ford.

Q. Who erected the first windmill in America?

A. George Yeardley.

Q. Booker T. Washington graduated with honors in three years from what Virginia school?

A. Hampton Institute, Hampton.

Q. In 1784 what boat designer and builder was granted a ten-year right to operate his craft on Virginia's waterways?

A. James Rumsey.

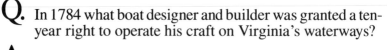

Q. Who was the original builder and owner of Robert E. Lee's Arlington House?

A. George Washington Parke Custis.

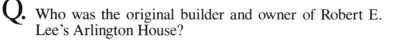

Q. Where did General Stonewall Jackson win his greatest victory of the War Between the States?

A. Chancellorsville.

Q. With the revocation of the London Company charter in June, 1624, what became the status of Virginia?

A. It became a royal colony.

Q. In 1647 an act against nonconformists caused many members of what religious group to leave Virginia and relocate in Maryland?

A. Puritans.

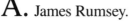

Q. What Virginian presided over the Whig Convention of 1839?

A. James Barbour.

Q. At what home did Patrick Henry and his family live after his political retirement?

A. Red Hill.

Q. What city was made the capital of the Confederate States of America on May 21, 1861?

A. Richmond.

———◆———

Q. In 1801 Meriwether Lewis served President Thomas Jefferson in what capacity?

A. As his private secretary.

———◆———

Q. From the original 500 colonists, to what number did Jamestown dwindle during the winter of 1609–10?

A. Sixty-five.

———◆———

Q. What railroad company in the 1880s laid the first railroad tracks down the Virginia peninsula?

A. The New York, Philadelphia & Norfolk Railroad.

———◆———

Q. The house where Stonewall Jackson died stands today on what battlefield of the War Between the States?

A. Fredericksburg.

———◆———

Q. The world's largest black congregation, the Abyssinian Baptist Church of New York, was largely the product of what Virginia-born individual?

A. Adam Clayton Powell, Sr.

———◆———

Q. What was the name of the 17,000-pound Union mortar used to lob 200-pound explosive shells into Petersburg?

A. "Dictator."

Q. At what plantation did the marriage of Anne Hill Carter and Governor Harry "Light Horse" Lee take place?

A. Shirley Plantation, Charles City County.

———◆———

Q. What Virginia governor received votes for President at the 1956 Democratic Convention?

A. John Battle.

———◆———

Q. Who built the Fredericksburg Rising Sun Tavern, often visited by George Washington, Thomas Jefferson, Patrick Henry, and the Lees of Virginia?

A. Charles Washington, youngest brother of George Washington.

———◆———

Q. King George III of England sold the Natural Bridge, including 157 acres, to Thomas Jefferson for what amount?

A. Twenty shillings.

———◆———

Q. In what home did Patrick Henry live during his most active political years?

A. Scotchtown.

———◆———

Q. What group of colonists, authorized to settle in southern Virginia, were blown off course and landed far to the north on December 11, 1620?

A. The Pilgrims.

———◆———

Q. The first Battle of Manassas, on July 21, 1861, was known to Northerners by what name?

A. Battle of Bull Run.

Q. James and Dolly Madison spent their honeymoon at what Shenandoah Valley estate?

A. Belle Grove Plantation.

———◆———

Q. To what political office was George Washington first elected in 1748?

A. He was elected by residents of Frederick County to serve in the House of Burgesses.

———◆———

Q. Who started the Cloverdale Furnace iron works in 1787?

A. Robert Harvey.

———◆———

Q. What two Virginians became the Whig party's first successful presidential and vice presidential candidates?

A. William Henry Harrison and John Tyler.

———◆———

Q. What canal, chartered by both Virginia and North Carolina, was completed in 1828?

A. The Dismal Swamp Canal.

———◆———

Q. What aged Indian leader led the massacre of 1644, resulting in the death of about 300 colonists?

A. Opechananough.

———◆———

Q. What President attended Christ Church Alexandria and has a pew commemorated to him?

A. George Washington.

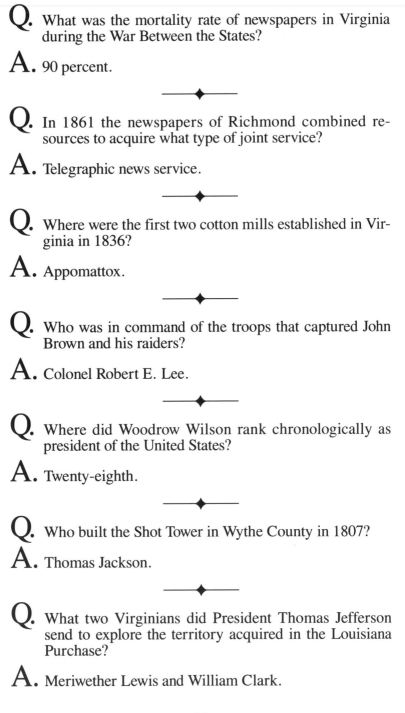

Q. What was the mortality rate of newspapers in Virginia during the War Between the States?

A. 90 percent.

━━━━◆━━━━

Q. In 1861 the newspapers of Richmond combined resources to acquire what type of joint service?

A. Telegraphic news service.

━━━━◆━━━━

Q. Where were the first two cotton mills established in Virginia in 1836?

A. Appomattox.

━━━━◆━━━━

Q. Who was in command of the troops that captured John Brown and his raiders?

A. Colonel Robert E. Lee.

━━━━◆━━━━

Q. Where did Woodrow Wilson rank chronologically as president of the United States?

A. Twenty-eighth.

━━━━◆━━━━

Q. Who built the Shot Tower in Wythe County in 1807?
A. Thomas Jackson.

━━━━◆━━━━

Q. What two Virginians did President Thomas Jefferson send to explore the territory acquired in the Louisiana Purchase?

A. Meriwether Lewis and William Clark.

Q. What Virginian became the nation's fourth president in 1809?

A. James Madison.

———◆———

Q. In opposition to the Stamp Act, what group met in Norfolk on March 31, 1766?

A. The Sons of Liberty.

———◆———

Q. The Iwo Jima Memorial was sculpted to honor what group of servicemen?

A. United States Marine Corps.

———◆———

Q. In what year did the University of Virginia become coeducational?

A. 1920.

———◆———

Q. Mary Jane Lumpkin donated what building in Richmond to be used as a school for blacks following the War Between the States?

A. Her husband's famous slave jail.

———◆———

Q. Where are George and Martha Washington buried?

A. On the Mount Vernon estate.

———◆———

Q. Who was the first appointed president of the Jamestown council?

A. Edward Maria Wingfield.

Q. What process did Chief Justice John Marshall establish to deal with the constitutionality of cases?

A. Judicial review.

———◆———

Q. Who led planters to meet at Leedstown on February 27, 1766, in opposition to the Stamp Act?

A. Richard Henry Lee.

———◆———

Q. What Virginia community was the only major loose leaf tobacco market before the War Between the States?

A. Danville.

———◆———

Q. Lord Dunmore's ships bombarded what city on New Year's Day, 1776?

A. Norfolk.

———◆———

Q. Who drew up the document called the Virginia Constitution of 1621?

A. Sir Edwyn Sandys.

———◆———

Q. What was designated to be the source of revenue for the first proposed colonial university in Virginia?

A. The Falling Creek iron foundry.

———◆———

Q. After the War Between the States, scientist Matthew F. Maury tried unsuccessfully to establish a colony of Virginians in what country?

A. Mexico.

Q. A monopoly on the sale of what imported product was granted by the English king to London Company in 1622?

A. Tobacco.

———◆———

Q. On what date did the first shiploads of permanent colonists arrive at Jamestown?

A. May 14, 1607.

———◆———

Q. Who was appointed as the first governor of the colony of Virginia?

A. Sir Thomas Gates.

———◆———

Q. What college for women opened near Amherst in 1906?

A. Sweet Briar College.

———◆———

Q. The resort of Rockbridge Baths sold for what amount of money in 1853?

A. $150,000.

———◆———

Q. What U.S. president assisted in the dedication of the George Washington Masonic National Memorial in Alexandria?

A. Herbert Hoover.

———◆———

Q. What Richmond shoe dealer was arrested in 1856 for shipping fugitive slaves to the north in shoe crates?

A. James A. Smith.

Q. What gifted orator moved the Virginia general assembly to pass the Virginia Resolves in reaction to the Stamp Act?

A. Patrick Henry.

———◆———

Q. What Virginia governor was the first black man elected governor of any state?

A. Douglas Wilder.

———◆———

Q. Founded at Lynchburg in 1893 by Methodists, what institution became the first fully accredited women's college in Virginia?

A. Randolph–Macon Womens College.

———◆———

Q. In what community in 1776 did Pastor Peter Muhlenberg preach his famous "Call to Arms" sermon?

A. Woodstock.

———◆———

Q. In 1831 what horse-drawn railroad became the first railroad to operate in Virginia?

A. The Chesterfield Railroad.

———◆———

Q. What famous American's initials are carved in the Natural Bridge?

A. George Washington.

———◆———

Q. Of whom did Robert E. Lee say, "He has lost his left arm, but I have lost my right arm"?

A. General Stonewall Jackson.

Q. What Virginia-born politician framed the Missouri Compromise?

A. Henry Clay.

Q. After defeating the Shawnee Indians in 1811, what nickname was given to William Henry Harrison, who later became the ninth U.S. president?

A. "Tippecanoe."

Q. What house museum displays Woodrow Wilson's Pierce-Arrow White House limousine?

A. Woodrow Wilson Birthplace in Staunton.

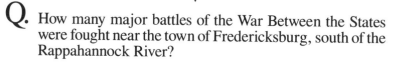

Q. Fielding Lewis and his wife, Betty, only sister of George Washington, had what Fredericksburg mansion built in 1752?

A. Kenmore.

Q. How many major battles of the War Between the States were fought near the town of Fredericksburg, south of the Rappahannock River?

A. Four.

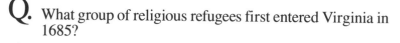

Q. Numerically, where does James Monroe rank as president?

A. Fifth.

Q. What group of religious refugees first entered Virginia in 1685?

A. French Huguenots.

Q. What famous Charlottesville tavern, now a restaurant and museum, welcomed patrons such as Jefferson, Lafayette, Madison, and Monroe?

A. Michie Tavern.

Q. Who was governor from 1641 to 1652?

A. Sir William Berkeley.

Q. Where on June 25, 1864, did approximately seven hundred old men and boys repel a Federal force of 2,000?

A. Staunton River Bridge.

Q. Who in 1683 declared that no one could operate a printing press in the Colony of Virginia?

A. King Charles II of England.

Q. At what home was Robert E. Lee born?

A. Stratford Hall.

Q. After covering the *Merrimac* with iron, Confederate forces gave it what new name?

A. The *Virginia*.

Q. On April 12, 1865, how many troops under General Robert E. Lee's command laid down their weapons at Appomattox?

A. 28,231 Confederate soldiers.

Q. Who presented the "Virginia Plan" at the Philadelphia Convention in 1787?

A. Virginia Governor Edmund Randolph.

Q. In 1628 the House of Burgesses achieved what success?

A. Royal recognition.

Q. What house of worship is the only colonial church in Virginia to have retained its original structure and furnishings?

A. Historic Christ Church, Lancaster County.

Q. Approximately how many Union and Confederate soldiers perished at the Battle of Chancellorsville in 1863?

A. 30,000.

Q. What young lawyer presented his first case, the "Parson's Cause," at the Hanover County Courthouse?

A. Patrick Henry.

Q. In 1974, Jay Winston Johns donated Highland, now called Ash Lawn, to what institute of higher learning?

A. College of William and Mary.

Q. In 1699 the capital of Virginia was moved to what location from Jamestown?

A. Williamsburg.

Q. What company completed the nation's first commercial canal in 1790?

A. The James River Company.

———◆———

Q. What black representative from Petersburg sponsored the bill to establish the first college for blacks in Virginia?

A. A. W. Harris.

———◆———

Q. What arsenal began supplying ordnance to the federal government in 1817?

A. Bellona Arsenal.

———◆———

Q. Mary Ball, mother of George Washington, was born in Lancaster County at what house?

A. Epping Forest.

———◆———

Q. On January 6, 1759, Martha Custis and George Washington were married in what colonial church?

A. Saint Peter's Parish, New Kent.

———◆———

Q. What Virginia courthouse contains the oldest continuous court records in the nation?

A. Eastville Courthouse, Northampton County.

———◆———

Q. In 1953 what former Virginia Military Institute cadet was the first professional soldier to be awarded the Nobel Peace Prize?

A. General George C. Marshall.

Q. Who did President Thomas Jefferson send to France to negotiate the Louisiana Purchase?

A. James Monroe.

Q. What United States naval vessel was captured by the British ship *Saint Domingo* in the Rappahannock River in June, 1813?

A. U.S.S. *Dolphin*.

Q. How many blacks won seats in the house of delegates in the 1867 election?

A. Twenty-one.

———◆———

Q. After the battles of Second Manassas and Chantilly, what famous nurse cared for wounded Union and Confederate soldiers in Saint Mary's Church?

A. Clara Barton.

———◆———

Q. What Virginia plantation is the only one in America owned by two United States presidents?

A. Sherwood Forest Plantation, owned by John Tyler and William Henry Harrison.

———◆———

Q. What Virginia-born U.S. president, who was elected in 1840, lived only thirty days after taking office?

A. William Henry Harrison.

———◆———

Q. What popular soft drink, developed in Waco, Texas, was named for a pharmacist in Rural Retreat, Virginia?

A. Dr Pepper, for Dr. Charles Kenneth Pepper.

Q. Where was Jefferson Davis imprisoned on May 22, 1865?

A. Fort Monroe.

Q. Under the Reconstruction Act, what designation was assigned to Virginia?

A. Military District No. 1.

Q. Who was the physician of Mary Washington whose apothecary shop may still be visited?

A. Hugh Mercer.

Q. In 1619 what group became the first democratically elected legislative body to meet in the New World?

A. The Virginia House of Burgesses.

Q. In the 1850s what Virginian was considered the South's wealthiest man, worth $4 million and owner of 3,000 slaves?

A. James Bruce.

Q. On what date did the Fifth Virginia Convention declare Virginia to be a free and independent state?

A. May 15, 1776.

Q. On August 18, 1930, what type of transportation was established to service Virginia?

A. Air passenger service.

Q. At what meeting did Patrick Henry make his famous "Give me liberty, or give me death" speech on March 20, 1775?

A. The Second Virginia Convention.

———◆———

Q. What two sections of the new state constitution, adopted on July 10, 1902, virtually eliminated the black vote in Virginia?

A. Poll tax and an "understanding clause."

———◆———

Q. By what title is John Smith's reply to the London Company's request for compensation known?

A. "Smith's Rude Answer."

———◆———

Q. What movement first developed in the early 1800s because of imbalances in political representation between the eastern and western areas of Virginia?

A. Sectionalism.

———◆———

Q. At the beginning of the War Between the States, how many miles of operating railroad tracks were there in Virginia?

A. 1,290.

———◆———

Q. What colonial school was proposed in 1618 to be established at Charles City Point?

A. The East India School.

———◆———

Q. What black teacher in Henrico County began a movement in 1906 to encourage vocational and industrial training?

A. Virginia Randolph.

Q. Under what famous frontiersman's direction was the Wilderness Road blazed through the Cumberland Gap in 1775?

A. Daniel Boone.

Q. What runaway slave from Norfolk became the first person arrested in a northern city under the Fugitive Slave Law of 1850?

A. Shadrach.

Q. What special role did the Wythe Union Lead Mine Company play during the War Between the States?

A. It was the chief domestic supplier of lead to the Confederacy.

Q. In 1778 Virginia became the first government in the world to outlaw what activity?

A. Slave trafficking.

Q. What agency was established in 1816 to supervise transportation enterprises on the state's waterways?

A. The Board of Public Works.

Q. Who led a slave rebellion across Southhampton County in August of 1831?

A. Nat Turner.

Q. Who proposed to the state legislature in 1831 that Virginia purchase all slave-born children?

A. Thomas Jefferson Randolph.

Q. In what two major Virginia battles did black troops participate during the War Between the States?

A. Battle of the Crater and the Battle of Fort Harrison at New Market Heights.

———◆———

Q. Who became the first governor of the Commonwealth of Virginia?

A. Patrick Henry, 1776–1779, 1784–1786.

———◆———

Q. Why was the early nineteenth-century Lynchburg mansion built by Dr. George Cabell, Sr., given the name Point of Honor?

A. Because of duels fought on its lawn.

———◆———

Q. Who started the Saint Paul Normal and Industrial School in Brunswick County in 1888?

A. The Reverend James S. Russell.

———◆———

Q. Concerning the fatalities of what battle fought on May 15, 1864, did General Grant exclaim, "The South is robbing the cradle and the grave"?

A. The Battle of New Market.

———◆———

Q. Who established Virginia's first successful smelting furnace in 1715?

A. Alexander Spotswood.

———◆———

Q. Following the War Between the States, what two northern philanthropies helped provide money and encouragement for black education?

A. The Freedmen's Bureau and the Peabody Fund.

Q. What World War II five-star general, famous for his "I shall return" statement, is buried in Norfolk?

A. General Douglas MacArthur.

◆

Q. Who became the first person to produce printing in Virginia in 1682?

A. John Buckner.

◆

Q. Under the prompting of Governor John Tyler, Sr., the general assembly established what educational entity in 1810?

A. The Literary Fund.

◆

Q. What "free" educational institution was established in 1634?

A. Syms Free School.

◆

Q. Who was appointed in 1730 by Governor Gooch as public printer for Virginia?

A. William Parks.

◆

Q. Called the "Apostles of Religious Liberty," Joseph Anthony, August Eastin, John Tanner, David Tinsley, Jeremiah Walker, and John Weatherford were imprisoned in what jail?

A. The old Chesterfield County jail.

◆

Q. What Virginian was chosen president of the First Continental Congress in September, 1774?

A. Peyton Randolph.

ARTS & LITERATURE

C H A P T E R   F O U R

Q. What Norfolk-born musician composed the swing tune "In the Mood"?

A. Joseph Copeland ("Joe") Garland.

Q. What Virginia resident painted the murals that adorn the walls of the Library of Congress?

A. Gari Melchers.

Q. What outdoor drama depicts the life of southwest Virginia mountain people during the coal boom?

A. *Trail of the Lonesome Pine*.

Q. In the 1860s Strasburg became well known for what type of earthenware?

A. Bell Pottery.

Q. What military melody, played at sunset, was composed in 1862 at the Berkeley Plantation?

A. "Taps."

Q. For whom was a new theater building in Richmond named in 1818?

A. Chief Justice John Marshall.

Q. What Virginia-born author won a Pulitzer Prize in 1923 for the novel *One of Ours?*

A. Willa Sibert Cather.

Q. Edgar Allan Poe's mother closed her professional acting career at what Richmond theater in 1811?

A. The Shockoe Hill Theater.

Q. What was the name of novelist Mary Johnston's Bath County home from 1913 until 1936?

A. Three Hills.

Q. Rainbow of Arts is held in what Virginia community?

A. Chesterfield.

Q. What Norfolk author wrote *Blood Tie* (1977) and *The Scapegoat* (1980)?

A. Mary Lee Settle.

Q. Who founded the monthly rural music publication *Musical Millions?*

A. Aldine Kieffer.

Q. The Virginia Museum of Fine Arts is home to several works by what noted Russian goldsmith?

A. Peter Carl Fabergé.

Q. From 1894 to 1913, where did John Fox, Jr., produce his romantic mountain novels?

A. Big Stone Gap.

Q. While a student at the College of William and Mary, Thomas Jefferson practiced three hours a day on what instrument?

A. Violin.

Q. Short story writer Peter Taylor of Charlottesville wrote what novel in 1950?

A. *A Woman of Means*.

Q. What Virginia theater ranks as the nation's oldest dinner theater?

A. Barksdale Theatre/Hanover Tavern.

Q. Edward Younger and James Tice Moore compiled what historical collection?

A. *The Governors of Virginia*.

Q. Where in Colonial Williamsburg may one see a collection of English and early American decorative arts?

A. DeWitt Wallace Decorative Arts Gallery.

Q. What society painter died at Charlottesville in 1936?

A. Prince Pierre Troubetzkoy.

———◆———

Q. On July 5, 1776, what Virginian proposed the design for the state seal?

A. George Mason.

———◆———

Q. What historical event including arts, crafts, and music is held each fall in Front Royal?

A. Festival of Leaves.

———◆———

Q. *The Blood of Paradise* was a 1979 novel written by what Fairfax resident?

A. Stephen Goodwin.

———◆———

Q. What city in Spotsylvania County is host to an annual photography exhibit and competition for amateurs?

A. Fredericksburg.

———◆———

Q. Fairfax resident Emily Pritchard Cary wrote what 1984 mystery novel?

A. *The Treasure of Juniper Junction*.

———◆———

Q. The Virginia chapter of the Victorian Society in America makes what Petersburg Federal mansion its headquarters?

A. Centre Hill.

Q. *Keeper of the Rules,* by Bruce J. Dierenfield, looks at the political maneuverings of what Virginia congressman?

A. Howard W. Smith.

Q. Where is the annual juried show of the Virginia Watercolor Society Exhibition held?

A. Lynchburg.

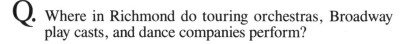

Q. What Canton-born author wrote many books on the subject of black history?

A. Carter G. Woodson.

Q. Where in Richmond do touring orchestras, Broadway play casts, and dance companies perform?

A. Carpenter Center for Performing Arts.

Q. Where is the Brush Mountain Arts and Crafts Fair held each year?

A. Blacksburg.

Q. How many volumes are maintained in the art reference library at the Virginia Museum?

A. 56,000.

Q. Who wrote the book *Historic Virginia Gardens?*

A. Dorothy Hunt Williams.

Q. Who was the sculptor of the Confederate memorial at Arlington?

A. Sir Moses Ezekiel.

Q. A museum honoring Edgar Allan Poe is in what city?

A. Richmond.

Q. Where was the first theater in America erected in 1716?

A. Williamsburg.

Q. What type of conveyance for wine bottles did Thomas Jefferson design into his dining room fireplace?

A. Dumbwaiter.

Q. Southwest Virginia provides what 1,000-seat musical performance facility for the preservation of traditional and bluegrass music?

A. The Carter Fold, Hiltons.

Q. What author, born in the Amelia County community of Dennisville in 1831, wrote under the pen name of Marion Harland?

A. Virginia Hawes Terhune.

Q. Where was the state's first public library established in 1794?

A. Alexandria.

Q. Norfolk's National Historic Wells Theatre is the home for what professional theater group?

A. The Virginia Stage Company.

———◆———

Q. What French artist created the statue of George Washington in the center of the Capitol?

A. Jean Antoine Houdon.

———◆———

Q. Historical novelist Mary Johnston was born in what community?

A. Buchanan.

———◆———

Q. What famous actress/writer was married at Christ Episcopal Church in the Warm Springs area of the Allegheny tier?

A. Cornelia Otis Skinner.

———◆———

Q. In what city is the Iwo Jima Memorial?

A. Arlington.

———◆———

Q. Who wrote the lyrics and composed the music to "Carry Me Back to Old Virginia"?

A. James A. Bland.

———◆———

Q. Who was the first professional painter in Tidewater Virginia?

A. Charles Bridges.

Q. What theater is designated the State Theatre of Virginia?

A. Barter Theatre.

Q. Vienna resident Elaine Moore authored what 1985 children's book?

A. *Grandma's House*.

Q. What Virginia building was the first in America to be built in the style of a classical temple?

A. Virginia State Capitol.

Q. *Guidebook to Virginia's Historical Markers* was compiled by what author?

A. Margaret T. Peters.

Q. The Virginia Museum of Fine Arts led the nation with what unique program to take art to the people?

A. Artmobiles.

Q. What Lynchburg native wrote the 1980 book *Listen, America?*

A. Jerry Falwell.

Q. What building, built in 1846, houses the Portsmouth Fine Arts Gallery?

A. The Old Court House.

Q. Pendleton Hogan describes the beauty and uniqueness of the University of Virginia in what book?

A. *The Lawn.*

Q. Strasburg presents what nationally acclaimed outdoor drama?

A. *The Passion Play.*

Q. Author William Styron was born in what Virginia city?

A. Newport News.

Q. What character actor was a native of Fairfax County?

A. George Fawcett.

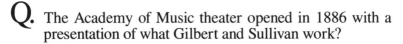

Q. The Academy of Music theater opened in 1886 with a presentation of what Gilbert and Sullivan work?

A. *The Mikado.*

Q. What is the official state song?

A. "Carry Me Back to Old Virginia."

Q. Illustrator Dugald Stewart Walker was a native of what Virginia city?

A. Richmond.

Q. Art in the Alley is an annual invitational exhibition in what town?

A. Salem.

Q. Who published Falmouth's first newspaper, *The Falmouth Advertiser,* in 1786?

A. Timothy Green.

Q. What Pulitzer Prize-winning columnist/author was born in Loudoun County?

A. Russell Wayne Baker.

Q. In what year was the Virginia Museum of Fine Arts established?

A. 1934.

Q. After what building was the Rotunda on the University of Virginia campus designed?

A. Rome's Pantheon.

———◆———

Q. Who designed the seal of Virginia?

A. George Wythe.

———◆———

Q. Where was the Academy of Sciences and Fine Arts of the United States founded in 1786?

A. Richmond.

Q. Who wrote *The Little Shepherd of Kingdom Come, Christmas Eve on the Lonesome,* and *Trail of the Lonesome Pine?*

A. John Fox, Jr.

Q. The stories about Walton's Mountain by Earl Hamner took place in what Virginia county?

A. Nelson.

Q. Who founded the *Richmond Enquirer* in 1804?

A. Thomas Ritchie.

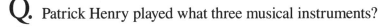

Q. Patrick Henry played what three musical instruments?

A. Violin, flute, and pianoforte.

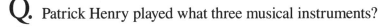

Q. What position did William Rufus Blake, Joseph Jefferson, and John Wilkes Booth hold at the Marshall Theater in Richmond?

A. Stage manager.

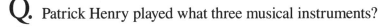

Q. What is the largest non-college library in Virginia?

A. The Virginia State Library, Richmond.

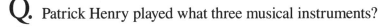

Q. What is the weight of the largest bell at the Luray Singing Tower, Luray Caverns?

A. 7,640 pounds.

Q. What was the location of the first theater building in Richmond that opened in 1786?

A. Shockoe Hill.

Q. Where was the pioneer black newspaper, *The True Southerner,* established in 1865?

A. Hampton.

Q. Painter George Caleb Bingham was born in what Virginia county?

A. Augusta.

Q. What former servant of Thomas Jefferson became bell ringer at the University of Virginia?

A. Henry Martin.

Q. Operating an advance base in Antarctica was the subject of what 1938 book by Richard E. Byrd?

A. *Alone.*

Q. What is the name of the oldest black weekly publication in the country?

A. Richmond *Afro-American.*

Q. Performances are given at which two theaters at Wolf Trap?

A. Filene Center II and The Barns.

Q. Who founded the black newspaper *The Afro-American Press,* in Lynchburg in the late 1880s?

A. I. Garland Penn.

Q. The Virginia Museum publishes what magazine?

A. *Arts in Virginia.*

Q. The dormitory room occupied by what famous writer is on permanent display at the University of Virginia?

A. Edgar Allan Poe.

Q. What organization was formed in Richmond in 1895 to foster native art?

A. The Art Club of Richmond.

———◆———

Q. How did the Barter Theatre receive its name?

A. During the Great Depression food was bartered for tickets.

———◆———

Q. What well-known actor made his American stage debut at the Marshall Theater in Richmond on July 13, 1821?

A. Junius Brutus Booth.

———◆———

Q. What internationally famous Swedish soprano appeared at the Marshall Theater in Richmond in 1850?

A. Jenny Lind.

Q. What Richmond poet, nominated for a Pulitzer Prize in 1981, wrote the collection of poetry titled *Everything Dark Is a Doorway?*

A. John Alspaugh.

———◆———

Q. What theatrical group was founded by the Virginia Museum in 1955?

A. The Museum Theatre Acting Company.

———◆———

Q. The Virginia Beach Arts Center hosts what annual outdoor art exhibit?

A. Boardwalk Art Show.

———◆———

Q. Vocal music teacher and songbook publisher Joseph Funk lived in what community during the first half of the 1800s?

A. Singer's Glen, near Harrisonburg.

———◆———

Q. Susan Mathias Smith of New Market wrote what 1982 children's book?

A. *No One Should Have Six Cats!*

———◆———

Q. The Chrysler Museum is internationally known for what 7000-piece collection?

A. The Institute of Glass.

———◆———

Q. What volume describes the harmony between President Jefferson and his Secretary of State, James Madison, in shaping domestic and foreign policies?

A. *The Papers of James Madison.*

Q. Lynchburg was the home of what famous black poet?

A. Anne Spencer.

Q. Fiction writer Robert Bausch of Fairfax authored what 1984 novel?

A. *The Lives of Riley Chance.*

Q. A Tudor-style mansion houses what Norfolk art museum?

A. Hermitage Foundation Museum.

Q. In what Henry A. Wise book is the Virginia Military Institute story told?

A. *Drawing Out the Man.*

Q. Bronze statues of both Captain John Smith and Dr. Hunter Homes McGuire were produced by what Norfolk-born sculptor?

A. William Couper.

Q. What play was performed at the inauguration of Williamsburg's second theater in 1751?

A. *Richard III,* by William Shakespeare.

Q. What is the world's largest musical instrument, found in the Cathedral Room of Luray Caverns?

A. The Great Stalacpipe Organ.

Q. With what musical did the Wells Theatre open in 1912?

A. Schubert's *The Merry Countess*.

———◆———

Q. What famous stained glass design firm created the windows of Saint Paul's Episcopal Church in Norfolk?

A. Tiffany.

———◆———

Q. The Sutherlin Mansion now serves the city of Danville in what capacity?

A. Museum of Fine Arts and History.

———◆———

Q. What song commemorates the Southern Railroad mail express train wreck at Danville in 1903?

A. "The Wreck of the Old '97."

———◆———

Q. Where in Richmond was John Vanderlyn's *Ariadne,* the first study of a nude, placed on public display?

A. The Virginia Museum.

———◆———

Q. The Pope-Leighey House of Mount Vernon was designed by what renowned architect?

A. Frank Lloyd Wright.

———◆———

Q. What Richmond native wrote a series of novels dealing with a romanticized place called Poictesme?

A. James B. Cabell.

Q. Hudgins resident Jane Flower Deringer penned what 1961 novel for young adults?

A. *The Puzzle Box Mystery*.

Q. The home and memorial gallery of artist Gari Melchers is in which historical community?

A. Fredericksburg.

Q. What Appomattox native originated the five-string banjo?

A. Joe Sweeney.

Q. A 300-year-old grist mill in Chesterfield County is the location for what entertainment facility?

A. Swift Creek Mill Playhouse.

Q. What artist in pastels produced many works in Norfolk, Suffolk, and throughout the Tidewater area between 1808 and 1811?

A. Felix Sharples.

Q. Stage and screen actor James Harlee Bell was born in what city in 1894?

A. Suffolk.

Q. What dramatic organization was formed in Richmond in 1918?

A. The Little Theater League.

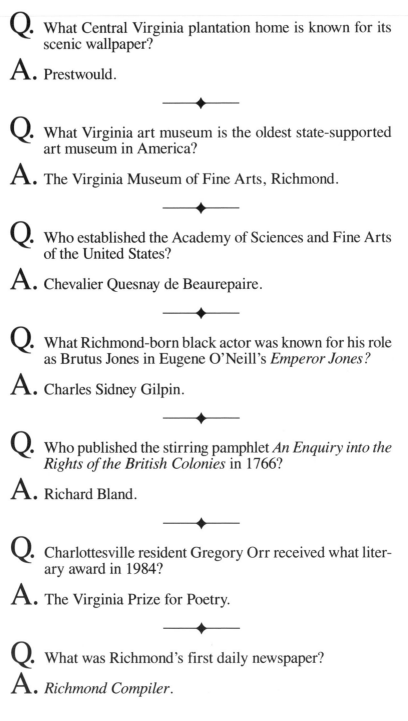

Q. What Central Virginia plantation home is known for its scenic wallpaper?

A. Prestwould.

———✦———

Q. What Virginia art museum is the oldest state-supported art museum in America?

A. The Virginia Museum of Fine Arts, Richmond.

———✦———

Q. Who established the Academy of Sciences and Fine Arts of the United States?

A. Chevalier Quesnay de Beaurepaire.

———✦———

Q. What Richmond-born black actor was known for his role as Brutus Jones in Eugene O'Neill's *Emperor Jones?*

A. Charles Sidney Gilpin.

———✦———

Q. Who published the stirring pamphlet *An Enquiry into the Rights of the British Colonies* in 1766?

A. Richard Bland.

———✦———

Q. Charlottesville resident Gregory Orr received what literary award in 1984?

A. The Virginia Prize for Poetry.

———✦———

Q. What was Richmond's first daily newspaper?

A. *Richmond Compiler.*

Q. Who came from Providence, Rhode Island, in 1872 to establish a music department at Hampton Institute?

A. Thomas P. Fenner.

◆

Q. What newspaper was founded in Williamsburg by William Parks in 1736?

A. *Virginia Gazette.*

◆

Q. Actor Wilton Lackaye was born in what county?

A. Loudoun.

◆

Q. The Collins Mediterranean Collection of Roman, Greek, and Egyptian artifacts is on permanent display at what art museum?

A. Roanoke Museum of Fine Arts.

◆

Q. What Richmond-born journalist wrote *The Kandy-Kolored Tangerine-Flake Streamline Baby* in 1965?

A. Tom Wolfe.

◆

Q. The marble statue of George Washington in the rotunda of the state capitol was executed by what French sculptor?

A. Jean-Antoine Houdon.

◆

Q. What German weekly newspaper started publication in the Shenandoah Valley in 1807?

A. *Der Virginische Volkberichter und Neumarketer Wochenschrift.*

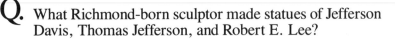

Q. What Richmond-born sculptor made statues of Jefferson Davis, Thomas Jefferson, and Robert E. Lee?

A. Edward V. Valentine.

Q. What famous novelist served as writer-in-residence for two years at the University of Virginia in the 1950s?

A. William Faulkner.

Q. Where did Edgar Allan Poe give his last public reading?

A. Exchange Hotel, Richmond.

Q. Virginia author William Hoffman penned what novel in 1985?

A. *Godfires*.

Q. The Old Pump House, Staunton, now houses what cultural display?

A. Staunton Fine Arts Center.

Q. What artist noted for his studies of the Army of North Virginia produced the bronze haut-relief entitled *The Color Bearer?*

A. William Ludwell Sheppard.

Q. Middletown in the Shenandoah Valley is home for what resident professional theater?

A. Wayside Theatre.

Q. What art and science museum was founded in Richmond in 1892?

A. The Valentine Museum.

———◆———

Q. Historical fiction writer Katie Letcher Lyle was a nominee in 1973 and 1974 for what American children's literature award?

A. The Newbery Award.

———◆———

Q. Landscapist and figure painter Elliott Daingerfield was born in what Virginia community?

A. Harpers Ferry.

———◆———

Q. What lawyer penned *The Letters of the British Spy* in 1803?

A. William Wirt.

———◆———

Q. Who was the gifted free black violinist of Charlottesville who, with his wife and three sons, entertained Lafayette at Monticello in 1825?

A. Robert Scott.

———◆———

Q. How many newspapers were in existence in Virginia at the close of the War Between the States?

A. Thirteen.

———◆———

Q. American realist painter Jerome Myers was a native of what city?

A. Petersburg.

Q. What renovated 1914 warehouse serves Roanoke as an arts and science performance complex?

A. Mill Mountain Theatre.

Q. What museum displays the famous Gilbert Stuart portrait of George Washington?

A. George Washington Masonic Museum.

Q. At what Alexandria shop do some 200 professional artists display and sell their creations?

A. Torpedo Factory Art Center.

Q. Radford stages what historical outdoor drama depicting the heroism of Mary Draper Ingles?

A. *The Long Way Home*.

Q. What noted portrait painter was born in Richmond in 1864?

A. Carle John Blenner.

Q. Williamsburg author Carol Clemeau Esler wrote what 1982 mystery novel?

A. *The Ariadne Clue*.

Q. What Staunton musical group is considered America's oldest continuously performing band?

A. Stonewall Brigade Band.

Q. What newspaper was established in Charlottesville in 1820?

A. *Central Gazette.*

Q. New York painter F. Graham Cootes was born in what Virginia town in 1879?

A. Staunton.

Q. Who was the editor of the Norfolk *Virginian Pilot* who received a Pulitzer award in 1929 for the year's best editorial?

A. Louis Isaac Jaffe.

Q. What Lexington outdoor theater has the unique setting of an old lime kiln?

A. Festival Theater at Rock Kiln Ruin.

Q. Orkney Springs is the site of what summertime musical event?

A. Shenandoah Valley Music Festival.

———◆———

Q. *Carry Me Back to Death* was a 1982 mystery/adventure novel by what Richmond author?

A. Robert P. Hilldrup.

———◆———

Q. What Richmond native painted the portrait of Jefferson Davis displayed in the Capitol in Washington, D.C.?

A. Augustus Lukeman.

Q. For what work did William Styron receive a Pulitzer Prize in 1968?

A. *The Confessions of Nat Turner*.

Q. What Richmond oil painter produced the work entitled *Sena Soma* or the *Sword Swallower?*

A. James Warrell.

Q. The Richmond Shockoe Hill Theater fire of 1811 claimed how many lives?

A. Seventy-three.

Q. In what Virginia community was Willa Cather born?

A. Gore.

Q. The Virginia Bookstore Award for best novel by a Virginia writer in 1980 was presented to what Fairfax resident?

A. Richard Bausch.

Q. What organization erected the Amelia County monument to poet and philosopher Father John B. Tabb?

A. Forest Memorial Association of Notre Dame, Indiana.

Q. The seven days of creation are presented at the Natural Bridge in what dramatic light display?

A. *Drama of Creation*.

Q. The Coastal Crafters Arts and Crafts Show may be seen in what Virginia town?

A. Charlottesville.

Q. What first novel brought William Styron into prominence?

A. *Lie Down in Darkness.*

Q. What Manassas resident and writer of novels for young people penned *Breakaway* and *Tough Is Not Enough* in 1981?

A. Ruth B. Hallman.

Q. The newspaper *True American* was established in what city in 1798?

A. Leesburg.

Q. What portrait painter, who produced many works in Virginia during the 1750s and 1760s, was dubbed by critics as "the almond-eyed artist"?

A. John Wollaston, Jr.

Q. The 1985 World of Poetry Golden Poet Award was given to what Arlington writer?

A. Mabel Ruth Bennett.

Q. What slave of Lord Botetourt in Williamsburg served as a fiddler at official state balls?

A. Sy Gilliat.

Q. What Williamsburg art facility houses the American folk art collection of Mrs. John D. Rockefeller, Jr.?

A. The Abby Aldrich Rockefeller Folk Art Center.

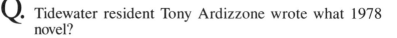

Q. Tidewater resident Tony Ardizzone wrote what 1978 novel?

A. *In the Name of the Father*.

Q. Romantic suspense author Phyllis Whitney now lives in what Virginia county?

A. Nelson.

Q. What wealthy planter, who built a beautiful home at West-over, kept a diary that gives modern readers a good picture of the life of the aristocracy of colonial Virginia?

A. A. William Byrd, II.

Q. What Petersburg church is one of only five buildings that have original Tiffany creations in every window?

A. Blandford Church.

Q. Christian Gehman of Richmond wrote what 1984 award-winning novel?

A. *Beloved Gravely*.

Q. What is the name of Hopewell's large arts and craft show and sale?

A. Hooray for Hopewell.

SPORTS & LEISURE

C H A P T E R   F I V E

Q. In 1973 what Thoroughbred was the first Virginia-bred-and-owned horse to win the Triple Crown?

A. Secretariat.

Q. What pitching star for the University of Richmond went on to play for the Boston and Milwaukee Braves?

A. Lew Burdette.

Q. The Natural Chimneys have been designated the location for what sports hall of fame?

A. The National Jousting Hall of Fame.

Q. In what stadium does Virginia Tech play its home games?

A. Lane Stadium.

———◆———

Q. The Virginia Lancers of the Atlantic Coast Hockey League have headquarters in what town?

A. Vinton.

Q. With a lifetime batting average of .262, what Richmond-born major league shortstop played in the 1950 World Series with the Philadelphia Phillies?

A. Granny Hamner.

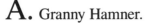

Q. What is the nickname of the University of Richmond teams?

A. Spiders.

Q. All-Pro Henry Jordan attended what Newport News high school?

A. Warwick High School.

Q. What museum houses the nation's most comprehensive collection of tobacco memorabilia?

A. National Tobacco–Textile Museum, Danville.

Q. The Virginia Military Institute practice field behind the stadium was renamed in 1985 to honor what man?

A. Dr. Martin D. ("Doc") Delaney, Jr.

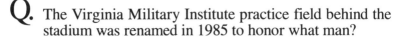

Q. What national class equestrian show offers the largest Grand Prix prize in the United States?

A. Roanoke Valley Horse Show.

Q. Kilts are worn at what July event in Alexandria?

A. Annual Virginia Scottish Games.

Q. What was the nickname of pitcher Charles Louis Phillippe, who was born in Rural Retreat?

A. "Deacon."

———◆———

Q. What ski resort hosts the Virginia Junior Alpine Championship?

A. Massanutten.

———◆———

Q. Charles McDaniel's University of Virginia record for most career solo tackles totaled how many?

A. 216.

———◆———

Q. In what community was athlete Bill McGarvey Dudley born on Christmas Eve, 1921?

A. Bluefield.

———◆———

Q. Chandler Harper was head pro at what Virginia golf course for seventeen years?

A. Glensheallah.

———◆———

Q. Virginia Military Institute's only undefeated, untied football team (1920 season) was known by what name?

A. "The Flying Squadron."

———◆———

Q. What famous Norfolk track star graduated in 1934 from the College of William and Mary?

A. Henry Moncure ("Monk") Little.

Q. During the 1956 season, what Covington native hit three home runs off of Whitey Ford in the second, fourth, and sixth innings in succession?

A. James Robert ("Jim") Lemon.

———◆———

Q. What University of Richmond four-sport letterman was selected Rookie of the Year in 1941 when he played for the Philadelphia Eagles?

A. Dr. Richard ("Dick") Humbert.

———◆———

Q. Over 100 horse-drawn vehicles are displayed in what Virginia museum?

A. Carriage Museum, Morven Park.

———◆———

Q. What Virginia Polytechnic Institute halfback played under the assumed name of Walter Brown in his early career because of his father's disapproval of football?

A. C. Hunter Carpenter.

———◆———

Q. Fredericksburg is the home of what antique aviation display?

A. Shannon Air Museum.

———◆———

Q. What nationally renowned horsewoman was named to the Virginia Sports Hall of Fame in 1976?

A. Jean McLean Davis.

———◆———

Q. What Virginia Sports Hall of Fame member, who was born in Galax, coached at Georgia Tech for twenty-two years?

A. Bobby Dodd.

Q. What museum houses a large array of military artifacts, including General George Patton's jeep?

A. U.S. Army Quartermaster Museum, Fort Lee.

Q. What Richmond native born in 1921 played eleven years with the New York Giants, Boston Braves, Cincinnati Reds, and Chicago White Sox?

A. Willard Marshall.

Q. In 1960 what alumnus of Hampden Sydney College took the head football coaching position there?

A. J. Stokeley Fulton.

Q. What Virginia athlete captained his 1916 football team, his 1915 basketball team, and his 1917 baseball team, and lost only one track race in his entire college career?

A. "Cy" Young.

Q. Lynchburg is the site of what annual internationally known road race?

A. The Virginia Ten Miler.

Q. In 1928 William and Mary selected what individual to become the athletic director, coach of five sports, and also serve as the athletic business manager?

A. William S. ("Pappy") Gooch.

Q. What fullback was voted Washington and Lee's Most Valuable Player in the fall of 1949?

A. Walt Michaels.

Q. What major league catcher was born in Charlottesville on November 19, 1942?

A. Larry Haney.

Q. The 1950 Washington and Lee University Generals played in what post-season bowl game?

A. The 1951 Gator Bowl.

Q. Chincoteague Island celebrates the talents of its craftsmen with what spring event?

A. The Easter Decoy Festival.

Q. Tennis great Arthur Ashe graduated from what Richmond high school?

A. Maggie Walker High.

Q. What Emory and Henry College basketball star was credited with being the first player at the school to use the present-day jump shot?

A. Glenn Roberts, Sr.

Q. "Bud" Metheny was selected the 1965 NCAA Coach of the Year while serving at what Virginia school?

A. Old Dominion University.

Q. In what area of the city does the Richmond Marathon begin and end?

A. Shockoe Slip at 12th and Canary streets.

Q. Don Strock of Virginia Tech established his professional career with what NFL team?

A. Miami Dolphins.

———◆———

Q. A history of Virginia Military Institute athletics is detailed in what book?

A. *The Corps Roots the Loudest.*

———◆———

Q. What Virginia Tech safety, honored in 1965 and 1966, was the school's only consensus football All-American?

A. Frank Loria.

———◆———

Q. Completing his athletic career at Duke University, Eric Tipton signed with what major league club?

A. Cincinnati Reds.

———◆———

Q. As of 1991, who has the best career shooting percentage in basketball at Washington and Lee University?

A. Frank Eppes.

———◆———

Q. What Virginian won the 1950 National PGA Championship.

A. Chandler Harper.

———◆———

Q. Since the establishment of University of Virginia football, what Virginia jerseys have been retired?

A. 24 (Frank Quayle), 35 (Bill Dudley), 48 (Joe Palumbo), 73 (Jim Dombrowski), and 97 (Gene Edmonds).

Q. In 1915 who became the only freshman at Davidson College to earn four varsity letters?

A. William Lee ("Monk") Younger.

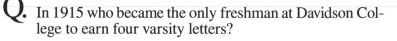

Q. Carroll Dale scored a touchdown in his very first game with what professional team?

A. Los Angeles Rams.

Q. Otis Douglas served as the 1931 football team captain for what school?

A. The College of William and Mary.

Q. Who served the University of Richmond as baseball coach for thirty-six years?

A. Coach "Mac" Pitt.

Q. In 1925 Joseph Chandler originated what track and field meet in which the best performer receives the coveted Chandler Award?

A. The Tidewater Relays.

Q. What sportswoman is the greatest woman tennis player Virginia has produced?

A. Penelope Anderson McBride.

Q. The one-and-one-half-ton gilded eagle figurehead from the U.S. Navy frigate *Lancaster* may be viewed at what Newport News museum?

A. The Mariners' Museum.

Q. Through the 1986 season, the football jerseys of what three Virginia Tech players have been retired?

A. 10 (Frank Loria), 78 (Bruce Smith), and 84 (Carroll Dale).

Q. Following a great football career at Virginia Tech, Bruce Smith joined what professional team?

A. Buffalo Bills.

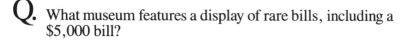

Q. What museum in Newport News is noted for its excellent collection of propaganda posters?

A. The War Memorial Museum.

Q. In 1892 Walter Camp named what Norfolk-born athlete to his squad, making him the first black player to play for him?

A. William H. Lewis.

Q. What museum features a display of rare bills, including a $5,000 bill?

A. The Federal Reserve Money Museum, Richmond.

Q. What Fredericksburg native, born in 1947, played thirteen years for the Baltimore Orioles?

A. Al Bumbry.

Q. Who was honored as Virginia Military Institute's first full-fledged All-American football player?

A. Jimmy Leech.

Q. What outstanding William and Mary athlete set a Southern Conference record in 1938 with a .572 batting average?

A. Arthur B. ("Bud") Metheny.

———◆———

Q. From 1950 to 1954 Norfolk-born George S. Hughes played for what professional team winning All-Pro honors?

A. Pittsburgh Steelers.

———◆———

Q. Of all the major golf classics, what tournament did Sam Snead fail to capture?

A. The United States Open.

———◆———

Q. In 1956 what former William and Mary fullback was named to coach the Norfolk Navy Tars?

A. Jack Cloud.

———◆———

Q. In 1985 what offensive tackle was the University of Virginia's first unanimous first-team All-American selection?

A. Jim Dombrowski.

———◆———

Q. Who was the tallest player on the 1986 Tech football roster?

A. Tight End Steve Johnson at six feet, six inches.

———◆———

Q. Rector Fieldhouse on the Virginia Tech campus acquired an indoor track from what New York facility?

A. Madison Square Garden.

Q. R. Walter Johnson, inducted into the Virginia Sports Hall of Fame in 1972, won how many tennis national championships?

A. Six.

Q. Who was the first Virginia Military Institute cadet to receive monograms in four major sports?

A. Francis Lee ("Frank") Summers.

Q. After Taylor H. Sanford completed his playing career, he scouted for what major league team?

A. New York Yankees.

Q. Tech coach H. M. ("Mac") McEver was inducted into the Virginia Sports Hall of Fame in what year?

A. 1980.

Q. What Virginia native became the National High Point Champion of the 266-cubic-inch Hydroplane Class in 1952?

A. Robert C. Rowland.

Q. After playing in the College All-Star game, Buster Ramsey signed with what professional team?

A. Chicago Cardinals.

Q. What Maggie Walker High School graduate was named 1972 NFL Man of the Year?

A. Willie Lanier.

Q. What community offers the Annual Hunt Country Stable Tour?

A. Upperville.

Q. Former Chicago Bear Beattie Feathers began his football career at Virginia High in what city?

A. Bristol.

Q. Player of the Year honors went to what Virginia Military Institute cadet selected to the 1986 All-Southern Conference basketball team?

A. Gay Elmore.

Q. *Sporting News* magazine named what Portsmouth native Minor League Executive of the Year in 1943?

A. Frank D. Lawrence.

Q. Richmond native Christopher T. Chenery established what 2,000-acre Thoroughbred race horse breeding and training ground?

A. The Meadow.

Q. Walt Michaels was named head coach of what NFL team in 1976?

A. New York Jets.

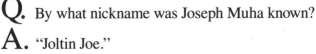

Q. By what nickname was Joseph Muha known?

A. "Joltin Joe."

Q. What athlete was the first world famous titlist to be inducted into the Virginia Sports Hall of Fame?

A. Arthur Ashe, Jr.

———◆———

Q. What Richmond native served as assistant football coach in 1932–1933 while attending law school at the University of Virginia?

A. William T. Thomas.

———◆———

Q. In later years what nickname was given to All-American Bill Dudley?

A. "Bullet."

———◆———

Q. What nationally famous "country spa" is in the scenic area of Hot Springs?

A. Homestead Hotel.

———◆———

Q. Jim Lemon managed what major league team in 1968?

A. Washington Senators.

———◆———

Q. What museum honors young Virginia Military Institute cadets who in 1864 aided distressed southern forces at the Battle of New Market?

A. Hall of Valor.

———◆———

Q. For what professional team did Walt Michaels play linebacker from 1952 until 1961?

A. Cleveland Browns.

Q. What Virginia Military Institute cadet was chosen for the 1985 All-Southern Conference football team?

A. Mike Mayo.

---◆---

Q. Hill Prince, owned by Richmond's Christopher T. Chenery, captured what high-stakes 1950 horse race?

A. Preakness.

---◆---

Q. What All-Southern Conference performer at William and Mary became a defensive coordinator for Calgary in the Canadian Football League?

A. Marvin Bass.

---◆---

Q. Morven Park houses a museum displaying exhibits of what sport?

A. Foxhounds and hunting.

---◆---

Q. "Cy" Young was a four-letter man at what Virginia university?

A. Washington and Lee University.

---◆---

Q. How many times did Henry Jordan receive All-Pro honors?

A. Seven.

---◆---

Q. What type of fish was caught at Wachapreagee, setting a 1984 saltwater all-tackle world record?

A. A twenty-one pound, eight-ounce Tautog.

Q. The Marine Corps maintains what museum at Quantico?

A. The Marine Corps Air–Ground Museum.

———◆———

Q. During the 1949 season, what William and Mary student set a school passing record with eighteen touchdowns?

A. Joseph ("Buddy") Lex.

———◆———

Q. In what city is the Virginia Sports Hall of Fame?

A. Portsmouth.

———◆———

Q. The year 1966 brought Tommy Scott to what NFL team as defensive coach?

A. New York Giants.

———◆———

Q. What Fredericksburg-born coach and official was enlisted to officiate the 1945 Alabama–Duke Sugar Bowl game?

A. George S. ("Gummy") Proctor.

———◆———

Q. In 1941 Arthur E. ("Art") Jones was a first-round draft choice of what NFL team?

A. Pittsburgh Steelers.

———◆———

Q. In 1966 what Martinsville-born major leaguer set the record for a catcher's rookie season by hitting nineteen home runs?

A. Cecil Randolph ("Randy") Hundley.

Q. What museum honoring one of its former graduates stands adjacent to the Virginia Military Institute?

A. George C. Marshall Museum and Library.

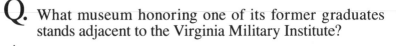

Q. Wrestling coach Billy Martin, Sr., led what Virginia high school to a dual match record of 259 wins and 9 losses?

A. Granby High School.

Q. What major league catcher, who was born in Franklin County, played twelve years for the New York Mets?

A. Ron Hodges.

Q. Who was the first small high school football player to make All-Tidewater in 1936?

A. Arthur E. ("Art") Jones, Suffolk High.

Q. What 1942 graduate, known at Virginia Military Institute for his musical as well as athletic abilities, joined the Philadelphia Eagles as an all-purpose running back?

A. Abisha ("Bosh") Pritchard.

Q. Athlete Clarence McKay Parker was given what nickname?

A. "Ace."

Q. What Virginia college is home to the stinging Wasps?

A. Emory and Henry.

Q. In 1940 what University of Richmond football player was the first player from Virginia selected to play in the College All-Star game in Chicago?

A. Edwin J. ("Ed") Merrick.

Q. What cave offers the only cavern elevator service in Virginia?

A. Shenandoah Caverns.

Q. After achieving athletic success and academic honors at the University of Virginia, what alumnus became medical director for the NFL for over ten years?

A. Dr. Harrison F. Flippin.

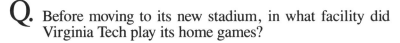

Q. In what city was Virginia Sports Hall of Famer Eric Tipton born?

A. Petersburg.

Q. Who is Virginia's all-time leading rusher with 3,237 yards?

A. John Papit.

Q. Before moving to its new stadium, in what facility did Virginia Tech play its home games?

A. Miles Stadium.

Q. In what year did Virginia Tech play its first home football game at night?

A. 1982.

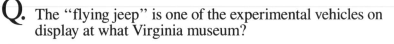

Q. The "flying jeep" is one of the experimental vehicles on display at what Virginia museum?

A. The U.S. Army Transportation Museum, Fort Eustis.

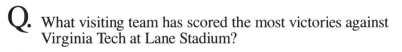

Q. What visiting team has scored the most victories against Virginia Tech at Lane Stadium?

A. Wake Forest.

Q. Where are the Casanova Hunt point-to-point horse races held?

A. Warrenton.

Q. What Lynchburg native amateur golfer has won the amateur championships of both America and Great Britain?

A. Vinny Giles.

Q. What Virginia Thoroughbred won the prestigious Kentucky Derby and the Belmont Stakes in 1972?

A. Riva Ridge.

Q. After ending his own career as a player, Bill Dudley coached what teams?

A. Yale, Virginia, and the Washington Redskins.

Q. In what community was pitcher Eppa Rixey born?

A. Culpeper.

Q. Who is the only Virginian to win the U.S. Open Golf Championship?

A. Lew Worsham.

Q. What former Virginia Tech leading receiver was named to the Football Foundation's College Football Hall of Fame in 1987?

A. Carroll Dale.

Q. What museum in Big Stone Gap depicts the life of its early pioneers?

A. Southwest Virginia Museum.

Q. During the 1953 season, who became the first University of Virginia athlete to earn All-American honors in two sports: lacrosse and football?

A. Thomas C. Scott, Jr.

Q. Majoring in physical education and sociology, Buster Ramsey graduated from what institute of higher learning?

A. The College of William and Mary.

Q. What Norfolk-born physician was personally responsible for shaping the careers of tennis pros Althea Gibson and Arthur Ashe?

A. R. Walter Johnson, M.D.

Q. Where is Rudolph Valentino's 1925 Rolls Royce displayed?

A. The Historic Car and Carriage Caravan at Luray Caverns.

Q. What mansion hosts the spring and fall steeplechase races of the Fairfax Hunt?

A. Belmont.

---◆---

Q. Willie Lanier, former middle linebacker of the Kansas City Chiefs, was born in what Virginia community?

A. Clover.

---◆---

Q. What Norfolk resident was the first duckpin bowling professional, giving exhibitions and playing match games?

A. Ida Simmons Slack.

---◆---

Q. What Virginia native was known as the funny man of his baseball era while at the same time batting over .300?

A. Walter Scott ("Steve") Brodie.

---◆---

Q. What Virginia school was one of only four ever to have its football team play in a bowl game, its basketball team compete in the NCAA tournament, and its baseball team win fifty games, all in one year?

A. Virginia Tech.

---◆---

Q. With what NFL team was Henry Jordan the first-round draft choice after his 1956 graduation from the University of Virginia?

A. Cleveland Browns.

---◆---

Q. In what Virginia city did Joseph H. ("Little Joe") Weatherly of NASCAR fame spend his school-age years?

A. Norfolk.

Q. What Hanover County native was the first president of the Southern Conference, as well as one of its founders?

A. C. P. ("Sally") Miles.

———◆———

Q. Coach William S. Jackson, inducted into the Virginia Sports Hall of Fame in 1979, was called by what nickname?

A. "Pedie."

———◆———

Q. Richmond's Ken Willard was the second leading ground gainer in the history of what NFL team?

A. San Francisco 49ers.

———◆———

Q. The College of William and Mary has what school colors?

A. Green, gold, and silver.

———◆———

Q. University of Virginia basketball star Rick Carlisle signed with what NBA team?

A. Boston Celtics.

———◆———

Q. What 1986 freshman Techman lived on campus as a baby with his mother and father while his dad finished his collegiate football career?

A. Ken Barefoot.

———◆———

Q. Tech played its first football game in what year?

A. 1892.

Q. While at William and Mary in 1939, Bob Rowland, noted speed boat racing champion, set what track and field record?

A. High hurdle record of 14.9 seconds.

————◆————

Q. What respected Culpeper native served as athletic director of Washington and Lee University from 1921 to 1954?

A. Richard A. ("Cap'n Dick") Smith.

————◆————

Q. What athlete was named to the Virginia Sports Hall of Fame in 1972 and was selected as a top scout for the San Francisco 49ers professional football team?

A. Clarence McKay Parker.

————◆————

Q. How many times did Sam Snead win the Masters Tournament and the PGA championship?

A. Three times each.

————◆————

Q. The 1975 National Football League Hall of Famer Roosevelt Brown was born in what city?

A. Charlottesville.

————◆————

Q. What Virginia Military Institute athlete was the first cadet to letter in four sports?

A. Paul C. Shu.

————◆————

Q. While playing basketball at Virginia in 1955, who led the state, the Atlantic Coast Conference, and the nation in scoring?

A. Richard ("Buzzy") Wilkinson.

Q. What Stuart native succeeded "Mac" Pitt at the University of Richmond, coaching baseball and basketball?

A. H. Lester Hooker, Jr.

———◆———

Q. The 1986 Tech vs. South Carolina football game was the first meeting of the two schools since what year?

A. 1974.

———◆———

Q. George Preas of Baltimore Colt fame won three state wrestling championships and was chosen All-American, All-Southern, and All-State while attending what Roanoke high school?

A. Jefferson High.

———◆———

Q. Inducted into the Virginia Sports Hall of Fame in 1978, what bowler was ranked the number one women's duckpin bowler in the nation, 1957–1958?

A. Doris Leigh.

———◆———

Q. George McQuinn wrote what instructional book for coaches?

A. *A Guide to Better Baseball.*

———◆———

Q. Norfolk's Leigh Williams earned four letters each in track, basketball, football, and baseball from 1927 to 1932 while attending what school?

A. Washington and Lee University.

———◆———

Q. When the American Football League was established, what William and Mary football star was selected as its first coach in 1960?

A. Garrard S. ("Buster") Ramsey.

Q. Who in 1985 became the first official honored by induction into the Virginia Sports Hall of Fame?

A. J. Dallas Shirley.

———◆———

Q. Virginia native Bob Porterfield played twelve years in the major leagues in what position?

A. Pitcher.

———◆———

Q. What Virginia Military Institute cadet holds the record for most points scored in his basketball career?

A. Ron Carter (2,228 points).

———◆———

Q. The football Hokies' selected what teammate as their 1985 Most Valuable Player?

A. Maurice Williams.

———◆———

Q. Tommy Thompson established his professional football career in 1949 with what team?

A. Cleveland Browns.

———◆———

Q. During the 1983 season, what nickname was given to the thunderous Tech tailbacks?

A. "The Stallions."

———◆———

Q. What fishing resort in Accomack County bills itself as the "Flounder Capital of the World"?

A. Wachapreague.

Q. What Virginia coach was the first high school coach in the nation to be named to the Helms Foundation Wrestling Hall of Fame?

A. Billy Martin, Sr.

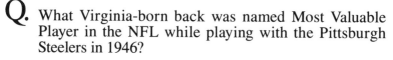

Q. What Virginia-born back was named Most Valuable Player in the NFL while playing with the Pittsburgh Steelers in 1946?

A. Bill Dudley.

Q. After completing his college career in 1943, what William and Mary athlete played professional football with the Richmond Rebels and professional basketball with the Richmond Barons?

A. Glenn C. Knox.

Q. What William and Mary graduate was All-Pro Linebacker in the NFL in 1952 and 1953?

A. Thomas W. ("Tommy") Thompson.

Q. Morven Park is host to what September vehicular sporting event?

A. Carriage Drive competition.

Q. Salem is the home for what Class-A baseball team?

A. The Redbirds.

Q. What Norfolk resident won the Hampton Championship of the Maury Regatta five successive years?

A. Charles ("Dink") Vail.

Q. What Hampton Institute athletic director was one of the original founders of the Central Intercollegiate Athletic Association?

A. Charles H. Williams.

Q. "The Galloping Ghost" was a nickname given to what Virginia Tech football player?

A. Alfred ("Al") Casey.

Q. Paeonian Springs is home to which museum featuring early farming techniques?

A. The Work Horse Museum.

Q. What Virginia-born pitcher was a five-time twenty-game winner in the National League?

A. Deacon Phillippe.

Q. What world championship-class golf course built by Chandler Harper was opened in 1955?

A. Bide-a-Wee.

Q. What Virginia resort has been listed among the top fifty tennis resorts in the nation by *Tennis Magazine?*

A. Boar's Head Inn and Sports Club.

Q. Who is said to be the best defensive guard ever to play for the University of Virginia?

A. Joe Palumbo.

Q. What Roanoke attraction displays the South's largest gathering of transportation artifacts?

A. Virginia Museum of Transportation.

◆

Q. Major league outfielder Willie Horton was born in what Virginia community?

A. Arno.

◆

Q. In the 1956 Olympics, what Arlington resident won the women's 100-Meter Butterfly in 1:11.0?

A. Shelley Mann.

◆

Q. Virginia Tech faced what opponent in its first night football game at home?

A. University of Virginia.

◆

Q. What former Warwick High School quarterback played for the Washington Redskins, Philadelphia Eagles, Minnesota Vikings, San Francisco 49ers, and the New York Giants?

A. Norman Snead.

◆

Q. What is the mascot for the University of Virginia?

A. The Cavalier.

◆

Q. What New York Yankee pitcher first showed signs of greatness at William and Mary College in 1941?

A. Victor ("Vic") Raschi.

Q. Otis Douglas played a total of four seasons for what NFL team?

A. Philadelphia Eagles.

Q. Where is the Sovran Bank 500 Grand National car race held?

A. Martinsville.

Q. Through the 1990 football season, Virginia Tech and the University of North Carolina have recorded how many scoreless ties?

A. Five.

Q. At what high school did Julius Conn coach track and basketball for over forty years?

A. Newport News High.

Q. With a lifetime average of .254, what Richmond native played eleven years with the Pittsburgh Pirates?

A. Gene Alley.

Q. Who coached Virginia Tech football from 1961 through 1970?

A. J. D. Claiborne.

Q. Where was major league outfielder Steve Brodie born?

A. Warrenton.

Q. At the end of the 1984 season, Tech's Bruce Smith won what award as America's top lineman?

A. Outland Trophy.

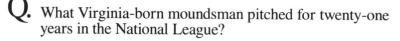

Q. What Virginia-born moundsman pitched for twenty-one years in the National League?

A. Eppa Rixey.

Q. Historical documents, arms and munitions, and memorabilia of the War Between the States are displayed in what Front Royal museum?

A. Warren Rifles Confederate Museum.

Q. What former University of Richmond graduate was named National Baseball Coach of the Year in 1955 as coach at Wake Forest?

A. Taylor H. Sanford.

Q. In what community was a 4-pound, 8-ounce, red ear sunfish caught setting a freshwater all-tackle world record?

A. Chase City.

Q. After his years at Virginia Tech, who became the first coach to win championships at three different high schools?

A. Karl Augustus ("Dick") Esleeck.

Q. After starring at the University of Richmond, what pitcher was selected Rookie of the Year in 1957 by *Sporting News* and the Baseball Writers Association?

A. Jack Sanford.

Q. In what football conference does Virginia Tech play?

A. Southern Independent Conference.

———◆———

Q. What Axton-born major league catcher played with the "Miracle Mets" in the 1969 World Series?

A. Joseph Clifton ("J. C.") Martin.

———◆———

Q. What Danville mathematics teacher produced state championship baseball teams for three decades?

A. Lawrence Girard ("Lefty") Wilson.

———◆———

Q. What Virginia Military Institute cadet was the number two choice of the Professional Football Association for best collegiate player in the nation, following Frank Sinkwich of Georgia?

A. Joseph Muha.

———◆———

Q. Richmond is home for what professional baseball team?

A. The Richmond Braves.

———◆———

Q. What Norfolk native became known as the "father of the Oyster Bowl"?

A. Melvin T. Blassingham, Sr.

———◆———

Q. What Virginia native received the Coach of the Year award from the National High School Coaches Association in 1968?

A. Julius ("Julie") Conn.

Q. At what Virginia high school was Roland C. Day a highly honored coach for twenty-eight years?

A. Petersburg High.

Q. How many of Virginia Tech's 1986 football opponents had head coaches who once coached at Tech?

A. Three: Clemson, Kentucky, and Temple.

Q. "Cy" Young is a member of how many sports halls of fame?

A. Three: Virginia, West Virginia, and National Football League.

Q. What are the official university colors of Virginia Tech?

A. Chicago maroon and burnt orange.

Q. In 1937 what Washington and Lee University student was named to the Helms Foundation All-American Basketball Team?

A. Bob Woods Spéssard.

Q. Where was golfing great Sam Snead born?

A. Ashwood, near Hot Springs.

Q. What nickname did legendary Walter Camp give to Virginia Tech football player Monk Younger?

A. "The Southern Panther."

Q. What mansion serves as the site of the International Equestrian Institute?

A. Morven Park near Leesburg.

———◆———

Q. Since the 1940s, who is the only Tech player to score on a pass reception, a punt return, a kickoff return, and an interception return during his career?

A. Billy Hardee.

———◆———

Q. What Hampton High School graduate became one of the stars of Virginia Tech's "Pony Express" backfield from 1925 through 1928?

A. Frank W. Peake.

———◆———

Q. What All-American center joined NBA ranks with the Houston Rockets after playing his last season for Virginia in 1983?

A. Ralph Sampson.

———◆———

Q. Which magnificent mansion hosts the Loudoun Hunt Spring Point-to-Point races?

A. Oatlands.

———◆———

Q. Melvin C. ("Meb") Davis coached what Dixie Professional Football League team?

A. Richmond Arrows.

———◆———

Q. With what team did Virginia Tech maintain its longest series of scheduled play?

A. The College of William and Mary (1928–1985).

Q. What Reedville native became the physical fitness consultant for the Cincinnati Reds in the spring of 1961, the year they won the National League pennant?

A. Otis Douglas.

Q. In the 1985 and 1986 basketball seasons, what six-foot, eleven-inch center for the University of Virginia won Most Valuable Player honors for leading his team in points and rebounds?

A. Olden Polynice.

Q. During the 1986 season, what woman University of Virginia basketball player set a school single-game record scoring thirty-three points?

A. Nancy Mayer.

Q. The Lynchburg championship "Mets" baseball club are in what league?

A. Carolina League.

Q. Bryce Resort, Basye, offers what two types of skiing?

A. Grass and snow skiing.

Q. The University of Virginia hosts its home football contests in what stadium?

A. Scott Stadium.

Q. The "Courtland Courier" was a nickname given to what University of Virginia football player?

A. James T. Gillette, Jr.

Q. Who took the helm as head football coach of Virginia Tech in 1978?

A. Bill Dooley.

———◆———

Q. The Virginia Lancers are at home in what sports complex?

A. The LancerLot.

———◆———

Q. What University of Virginia athlete was recognized as the South's first All-American, playing on Walter Camp's 1915 team?

A. Eugene Noble ("Buck") Mayer.

———◆———

Q. What major league outfielder, who was born in Richmond on August 4, 1948, played with Detroit in the 1984 World Series?

A. Johnny Grubb.

———◆———

Q. The War Between the States is simulated annually at what June event in Alexandria?

A. The Civil War Reenactment Weekend.

———◆———

Q. In what two years did Virginia Tech football enjoy undefeated seasons?

A. 1918 (7–0) and 1954 (8–0–1).

———◆———

Q. In his first season at Emory and Henry College in 1927, what beloved coach produced a winning football record of 9–0?

A. William S. Jackson.

Q. What Virginia Tech football coach and athletic director was known for his major fund-raising efforts, that expanded the school's athletic program?

A. Frank O. Moseley.

———◆———

Q. Thanksgiving Hunt Weekend at Charlottesville centers around what unusual event?

A. "Blessing of the Hounds."

———◆———

Q. Bob Davis set a record in 1964 for Virginia's longest running play, carrying the ball how many yards?

A. Eighty-eight yards for a touchdown.

———◆———

Q. A willing wind and eager contestants make what May event at Ashlawn-Highland a special happening?

A. Kite Day.

———◆———

Q. Tech football players first wore the official school colors in what year?

A. 1896.

———◆———

Q. What Caroline County native is credited with introducing swimming to Old Dominion University?

A. Joseph C. ("Scrap") Chandler.

———◆———

Q. Wayne Morrison holds the University of Virginia scoring record for most career field goals, totaling how many?

A. Thirty-eight.

Q. What Virginia-born first baseman hit .438 playing with the St. Louis Browns in the 1944 World Series?

A. George McQuinn.

———◆———

Q. Virginia Tech has inducted what three coaches into the University's Sports Hall of Fame?

A. Frank O. Moseley, C. P. Miles, and H. B. Redd.

———◆———

Q. What unique spring relay race by land and water is held at Lexington?

A. The Road and River Relay.

———◆———

Q. In 1930–1931, what University of Virginia student was considered the best all-around athlete in the state?

A. J. C. Herbert Bryant.

———◆———

Q. What all-around athlete at Fredericksburg High, and later at the University of Richmond, was the first American to be awarded the Council International Sports Militaire Medal of Honor?

A. Stuart W. ("Stukie") Hoskins.

———◆———

Q. Skeet shooting, falconry, and working dog demonstrations are all a part of what September event in Midlothian?

A. National Hunting and Fishing Day.

———◆———

Q. What former team member served as Rookie Coach of the Virginia Lancers during the 1986–1987 season?

A. John ("Torty") Tortorella.

SCIENCE & NATURE

C H A P T E R   S I X

Q. What two national forests are in Virginia?

A. The George Washington and Jefferson national forests.

———◆———

Q. Where were the first seven United States astronauts trained?

A. The NASA Langley Space Center, Hampton.

———◆———

Q. What geological formation in Virginia is listed as one of the Seven Natural Wonders of the World?

A. The Natural Bridge.

———◆———

Q. In 1974 what became the official state shell?

A. The oyster shell.

———◆———

Q. What is Virginia's most valuable mineral resource?

A. Coal.

Q. What is the depth of the water along the route of the Chesapeake Bay Bridge–Tunnel?

A. Twenty-five to one hundred feet.

Q. Of the hardwoods in the state, which is the most important for lumber?

A. Oak.

Q. To what Virginia record low did the temperature plunge at Monterey on February 10, 1899?

A. -29° F.

Q. Shenandoah Caverns are famous for what formations that have been featured in *National Geographic Magazine?*

A. Bacon formations.

Q. Measuring only two inches in length when full grown, what is the smallest salamander in Virginia?

A. The pigmy salamander.

Q. What Middletown artisan was noted for his precision compasses?

A. Jacob Danner.

Q. Where is the Presquile National Wildlife Refuge?

A. On an island in the James River.

Q. Virginia established a program in 1976 to attempt to re-introduce what swift-flying predatory bird into the wilds of the Commonwealth?

A. Peregrine falcon.

Q. Bear Creek Lake occupies the heart of what state forest?

A. Cumberland State Forest.

Q. How many licensed wineries operate within the Commonwealth of Virginia?

A. Twenty-nine.

Q. Of the various sea turtles found in Chesapeake Bay, what variety is most common?

A. Loggerhead.

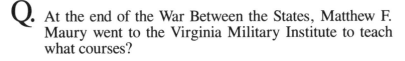

Q. At the end of the War Between the States, Matthew F. Maury went to the Virginia Military Institute to teach what courses?

A. Meteorology and astronomy.

Q. The Assateague Lighthouse can be seen for how many nautical miles?

A. Nineteen.

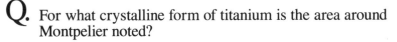

Q. For what crystalline form of titanium is the area around Montpelier noted?

A. Rutile.

Q. Where does the world's largest film projector bring visitors into the picture?

A. Science Museum of Virginia, Richmond.

———◆———

Q. What large salamander found in the coastal area of Virginia has gills and forelegs, but no hindlegs?

A. The greater siren salamander.

———◆———

Q. What snake found in the southwestern Piedmont areas of Virginia is mildly poisonous to prey, but not harmful to humans?

A. Southeastern crowned snake.

———◆———

Q. How many of Virginia's state parks offer saltwater fishing?

A. Six.

———◆———

Q. Displays of maple syrup production may be seen at what Virginia event?

A. The Highland County Maple Festival.

———◆———

Q. What is the largest and fiercest member of the owl family found in Virginia?

A. The great horned owl.

———◆———

Q. What Roanoke County inventor patented a cigarette-manufacturing machine in 1881?

A. James Bonsack.

Q. What Tidewater community is the soft-shell crab capital of the United States?

A. Tangier Island.

Q. The wild turkey of Virginia can run at what speed?

A. Fifteen miles per hour.

Q. One of the rarest and most unusual North American land snails, the Virginia fringed mountain snail, thus far has been found only in what county?

A. Pulaski.

Q. A canal boat ride through the beauty of nature is offered at what Norfolk attraction?

A. Norfolk Botanical Gardens.

Q. What museum featuring displays on shellfish farming also depicts the history of Chincoteague?

A. The Oyster Museum.

Q. What bird serves as a symbol for the city of Bristol?

A. The native redtail hawk.

Q. Where is the only research collection and educational center for the natural sciences in Virginia?

A. Martinsville, Virginia Museum of Natural History.

Q. What is the state bird of Virginia?

A. Cardinal.

———◆———

Q. From 1928 through 1957 Richard E. Byrd was instrumental in guiding the explorations of what continent?

A. Antarctica.

———◆———

Q. Fire-cured tobacco is used primarily in what two products?

A. Snuff and chewing tobacco.

———◆———

Q. Who was known as the "African calculator" of Alexandria?

A. Thomas Fuller.

———◆———

Q. How many Wildlife Management Areas are within Virginia?

A. Twenty-six.

———◆———

Q. The seafaring town of Chincoteague first became famous for what variety of seafood?

A. Salt oysters.

———◆———

Q. What is the average altitude of the Blue Ridge Parkway?

A. 3,000 feet above sea level.

Q. What three poisonous snakes are indigenous to Virginia?

A. Copperhead, cottonmouth, and rattlesnake.

Q. Wythe County is noted for what two metal deposits?

A. Lead and zinc.

Q. Virginia is one of the leading producers of what types of seafood?

A. Crab and oysters.

Q. Who predicted and discovered the existence of Skyline Caverns in 1937?

A. Walter S. Amos.

Q. What mammal, belonging to the order of Marsupialia and having a grasping tail, is common in Virginia?

A. The Virginia gray opossum.

Q. The famous pony swim and auction on Chincoteague Island takes place the last Wednesday and Thursday of what month?

A. July.

Q. Where is the Mid-Atlantic Wildfowl festival held?

A. Virginia Beach.

Q. Virginian Matthew Fontaine Maury conceived the idea of what intercontinental communication system?

A. The trans-Atlantic cable.

Q. What is Virginia's most important big game animal?

A. The Virginia white-tailed deer.

Q. In addition to timber and canebrake rattlesnake, what two other types of poisonous snakes are found in Virginia?

A. Northern copperhead and eastern cottonmouth.

Q. The Wash Woods Environmental Education Center is in what state park?

A. False Cape State Park.

Q. What timepiece designed by Thomas Jefferson still marks the hours in the entrance hall of Monticello?

A. The seven-day calendar clock.

Q. What two types of vultures may be found in the Commonwealth of Virginia?

A. Black and turkey vultures.

Q. What Virginia Beach pilot built and flew a replica of the Wright Brothers' first successful airplane in 1978?

A. Ken Kellett.

Q. Virginia is famous for what pork product?

A. Smithfield hams.

———◆———

Q. Who brought from Europe to Williamsburg in 1773 10,000 wine grape cuttings, 4,000 olive and lemon trees, and silkworms?

A. Filippo Mazzei.

———◆———

Q. What is the most common nonpoisonous snake in Virginia?

A. Black snake.

———◆———

Q. How many pounds of tobacco were exported by the Virginia colony in 1755?

A. More than forty-two million.

———◆———

Q. The Roanoke Valley Science Museum and Planetarium are in what multimillion dollar complex?

A. Center in the Square.

———◆———

Q. What rare formations in the Grand Caverns, Grottoes, remain a mystery to geologists?

A. Shield formations.

———◆———

Q. What makes up about two-thirds of a bobcat's diet in Virginia?

A. Rabbits.

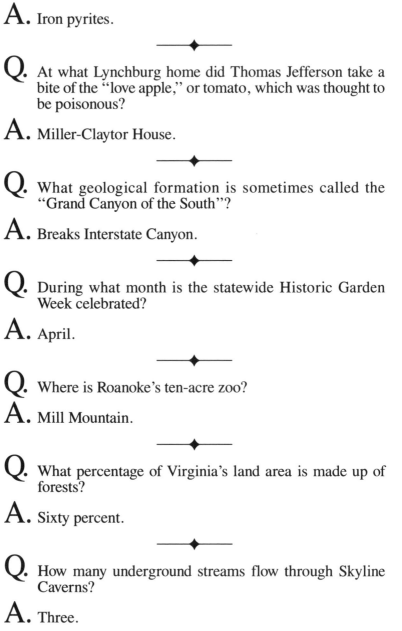

Q. In the last half of the nineteenth century and the early years of the twentieth, what material was mined and smelted at Mineral to produce sulphur?

A. Iron pyrites.

———◆———

Q. At what Lynchburg home did Thomas Jefferson take a bite of the "love apple," or tomato, which was thought to be poisonous?

A. Miller-Claytor House.

———◆———

Q. What geological formation is sometimes called the "Grand Canyon of the South"?

A. Breaks Interstate Canyon.

———◆———

Q. During what month is the statewide Historic Garden Week celebrated?

A. April.

———◆———

Q. Where is Roanoke's ten-acre zoo?

A. Mill Mountain.

———◆———

Q. What percentage of Virginia's land area is made up of forests?

A. Sixty percent.

———◆———

Q. How many underground streams flow through Skyline Caverns?

A. Three.

Q. What was the primary cause of the rapid decline of the bald eagle in the Commonwealth during the 1960s?

A. Extensive use of DDT and similar pesticides.

Q. Measuring roughly 100 feet in diameter, the Natural Tunnel in Scott County is what length?

A. Nearly 900 feet.

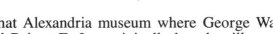

Q. What variety of crab is featured at the annual Crab Carnival in West Point?

A. Blue crab.

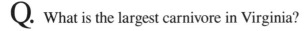

Q. What Alexandria museum where George Washington and Robert E. Lee originally bought pills and potions may be visited today?

A. The Stabler-Leadbeater Apothecary Shop.

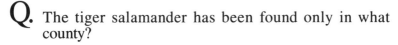

Q. Protected by federal law, the yellowfin mad tom in Virginia is now found in only what stream?

A. Copper Creek, in Scott and Russell counties.

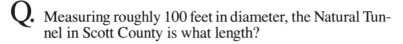

Q. What is the largest carnivore in Virginia?
A. The black bear.

Q. The tiger salamander has been found only in what county?

A. York.

Q. What type of relatively hard coal is found in Montgomery and Pulaski counties?

A. Semianthracite.

Q. Who compiled the booklet on sea turtles entitled *The Marine Turtles of Virginia, with Notes on Identification and Natural History?*

A. Dr. Jack A. Musick.

Q. What town established in 1811 became the terminus of the James River and Kanawha Canal?

A. Buchanan.

Q. At Langley Research Center what are the highest wind speeds that wind tunnels can produce?

A. In excess of 15,000 miles per hour.

Q. What kind of large salamander found in Virginia grows up to forty inches in length?

A. The Two-toed amphiuma.

Q. How many recreational state parks are there in the Commonwealth of Virginia?

A. Twenty-three.

Q. How tall are the towering limestone structures in Natural Chimneys Regional Park?

A. 120 feet high.

Q. What aircraft is on display at the Science Museum of Virginia in Richmond?

A. Solar Challenger.

Q. What tree, noted for its "knees," is found in the swamp areas of Virginia?

A. Cypress.

Q. What event takes place on Chincoteague Island every Thanksgiving weekend?

A. Waterfowl Open House.

Q. Ferrum is host to what unique equestrian celebration?

A. Blue Ridge Draft Horse and Mule Show.

Q. What colorful red, black, and yellow (or white) banded snake is found in the extreme southeastern corner of the state?

A. Scarlet king snake.

Q. How many species of birds visit the Chincoteague Wildlife Refuge annually?

A. Over 260.

Q. In the Great Dismal Swamp area, what beverage was at one time believed to give immunity to malaria?

A. Juniper tea.

Q. Schuyler has long been known for what type of mineral?

A. Soapstone.

Q. A rare white rhino is an attraction at what Tidewater zoo?

A. Lafayette Zoological Park.

Q. What do Tidewater crabmen call crabs that are in the process of shedding their old shells?

A. "Peelers."

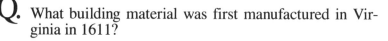

Q. The Goshen Pass Natural Area is on the southwest face of what mountain?

A. Little North Mountain.

Q. What building material was first manufactured in Virginia in 1611?

A. Bricks.

Q. What is the state flower of Virginia?

A. Flowering dogwood.

Q. Approximately how many deer are bagged annually by Virginia bow hunters?

A. One thousand.

Q. The cultivation of what crop was introduced to the colonists in 1612?

A. Tobacco.

Q. What Virginia-born scientist became known as the "Pathfinder of the Seas"?

A. Matthew Fontaine Maury.

Q. Most of Virginia's reserves are made up of what type of coal?

A. Bituminous.

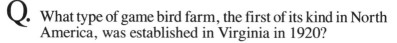

Q. What state agency regulates game bag limits, along with hunting and fishing regulations, in the Commonwealth of Virginia?

A. Commission of Game and Inland Fisheries.

Q. What type of game bird farm, the first of its kind in North America, was established in Virginia in 1920?

A. A quail farm.

Q. The Chesapeake Bay Bridge–Tunnel required the construction of how many islands.

A. Four.

Q. The Virginia Marine Science Museum is in what city?

A. Virginia Beach.

Q. What three species of bats are endangered in the Commonwealth?

A. The Indiana, gray, and Virginia big-eared bats.

Q. What famous sea explorer chose Norfolk as home base for his society headquarters?

A. Captain Jacques-Yves Cousteau.

Q. Children may produce their own television shows at what Newport News living museum?

A. The Nature and Science Center.

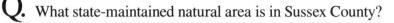

Q. What is the name of Virginia's largest vineyard, situated on 110 acres near Culpeper?

A. Prince Michel Vineyard.

Q. What institute of higher learning houses the Medical College of Virginia?

A. Virginia Commonwealth University.

Q. What state-maintained natural area is in Sussex County?

A. The Charles C. Steirly Heron Rookery.

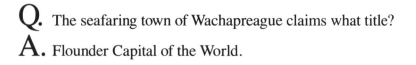

Q. The seafaring town of Wachapreague claims what title?

A. Flounder Capital of the World.

Q. What state park features hiking trails to the summit of Haw Orchard Mountain?

A. Grayson Highlands State Park.

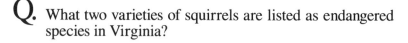

Q. Smithfield hams are processed from hogs fed on what feed?

A. Peanuts.

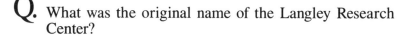

Q. What two varieties of squirrels are listed as endangered species in Virginia?

A. Delmarva fox squirrel and northern flying squirrel.

Q. Virginia Tech is one of few schools nationwide to offer a degree in what science?

A. Doctor of Veterinary Medicine.

Q. What was the original name of the Langley Research Center?

A. Langley Memorial Aeronautical Laboratory.

Q. How many species and subspecies of snakes exist in Virginia?

A. Thirty-six.

Q. Where is the only exhibition coal mine in the world through which visitors can drive their cars?

A. Pocahontas Exhibition Coal Mine.

Q. What agrarian organization did John Taylor found in 1817?

A. The Agricultural Society of Virginia.

———◆———

Q. What noted psychic died at Virginia Beach in 1945?

A. Edgar Cayce.

———◆———

Q. Oak Grove is noted for what 36,000-gallon capacity winery?

A. The Ingleside Plantation Vineyards.

———◆———

Q. What waterfall attracts visitors to Nelson County?

A. Crabtree Falls.

———◆———

Q. By what other name is the John H. Kerr Reservoir known?

A. Buggs Island Lake.

———◆———

Q. What invention was patented in 1826 by Louisa County resident Edmund Pendleton?

A. A tobacco drying and curing kiln.

———◆———

Q. The Portsmouth Museums System displays what 1915 U.S. Coast Guard navigational aid?

A. The Portsmouth Lightship.

Q. What Rockbridge County-born Virginian invented the "twisted loop rotary hook sewing machine" in 1857?

A. James Ethan Allen Gibbs.

———◆———

Q. How many species of endangered mussels may be found in the Tennessee River drainage area in Virginia?

A. Nine.

———◆———

Q. What Virginia community calls itself the "Clam Capital of the World"?

A. Chincoteague.

———◆———

Q. The moon-walking suit of what Apollo 15 astronaut is on display at Langley Research Center?

A. David Scott.

———◆———

Q. What rare and endangered isopod is found in only one cave system in Virginia?

A. The Madison Cave isopod.

———◆———

Q. The fifty-acre lake at Douthat State Park is stocked with what type of fish?

A. Trout.

———◆———

Q. What is the oldest piece of edible cured meat in existence, cured in 1902 at Smithfield?

A. Mr. P. D. Gwaltney, Jr.'s Pet Ham.

Q. What clan-colonizing woodpecker is listed as endangered and facing extinction in Virginia because of loss of necessary habitat?

A. The red-cockaded woodpecker.

Q. The transloader of the Westmoreland Coal Company at the Bullitt Mine Complex, Appalachia, processes how many tons of goal annually?

A. Four to five million.

Q. What is the only county in which the mountain earth snake has been found?

A. Highland.

Q. What Virginia cave houses the fifty-seven-ton Wedding Bell formation?

A. Dixie Caverns, Roanoke–Salem.

Q. At what farm near Raphine may one view the processing of wool into yarn?

A. Chester Farms.

Q. What domestic animal was introduced into Virginia in 1610?

A. The horse.

Q. What two writers have teamed up to compile in-depth field guides to Virginia trees, shrubs, and wildflowers?

A. Oscar W. Gupton and Fred C. Swope.

Q. What Tazewell-born physician and medical educator is credited with performing the first antiseptic operation in Virginia?

A. Dr. George Ben Johnston.

Q. Approximately how many pounds of rainbow trout does the Wytheville State Fish Hatchery produce each year?

A. 150,000.

Q. What state agency is responsible for Virginia's state parks?

A. Virginia Division of Parks and Recreation.

Q. How many species of freshwater mussels occur in Virginia?

A. Sixty-five.

Q. What upper Shenandoah Valley museum displays Indian artifacts between eleven and twelve thousand years old?

A. Thunderbird Museum.

Q. Who first planted tobacco in Virginia?

A. John Rolfe.

Q. What 1938 Public Works Administration project created power for Danville?

A. The Pinnacles Hydroelectric Development.

Q. What is the smallest mammal found in Virginia?

A. The short-tailed shrew.

———◆———

Q. Excluding cigars, what portion of the nation's tobacco goods were being produced in Virginia in 1840?

A. Forty-one percent.

———◆———

Q. What are mature male crabs called by Tidewater crabmen?

A. "Jimmies."

———◆———

Q. How many acres are designated as national forest in the Commonwealth of Virginia?

A. One and one-half million.

———◆———

Q. What type of mineral formation gave Fairy Stone State Park its name?

A. Staurolite Crystals.

———◆———

Q. In what portion of the state is the smooth green snake found?

A. Only in the extreme western part.

———◆———

Q. The Delmarva fox squirrel has been successfully reintroduced into what wildlife refuge from Maryland stock?

A. The Chincoteague National Wildlife Refuge.

Q. What is the official Virginia state tree?

A. Flowering dogwood, also the state flower.

———◆———

Q. What colonial leader introduced a herd of blooded cattle to America and stressed soil fertilization?

A. George Yeardley.

———◆———

Q. What small oriental elk is found in the Chincoteague Wildlife Refuge?

A. Sika deer.

———◆———

Q. In what land region is the majority of the state's tobacco grown?

A. The Piedmont.

———◆———

Q. What Virginian, born at Mill Hill in 1754, is noted in the field of agriculture for his work in soil improvement and crop rotation?

A. John Taylor.

———◆———

Q. At what geological formations are jousting tournaments held annually?

A. Natural Chimneys, Shenandoah Valley.

———◆———

Q. What colorful fowl roam the grounds of James Monroe's home Ash Lawn?

A. Peacocks.

Q. In 1966 the legislature chose what dog as the official state dog?

A. The American foxhound.

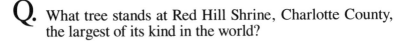

Q. What is the main use of Virginia's flue-cured tobacco?

A. Domestic cigarette production.

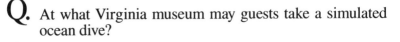

Q. Skyline Caverns is the only place in the world where what type of formations may be viewed?

A. Anthodites.

Q. What tree stands at Red Hill Shrine, Charlotte County, the largest of its kind in the world?

A. Osage orange tree.

Q. At what Virginia museum may guests take a simulated ocean dive?

A. Virginia Marine Science Museum.

Q. Inventor Cyrus McCormick was born in what Virginia county?

A. Rockbridge.

Q. What community is the Apple Capital of Virginia?

A. Winchester.

Q. What high tech television network is based in Virginia Beach?

A. The Christian Broadcasting Network.

———◆———

Q. How many pounds of tobacco were harvested in Virginia in 1989?

A. 93,184,000.

———◆———

Q. What Virginia county is among the nation's leaders in turkey production?

A. Rockingham.

———◆———

Q. In what year did Virginia's state parks first open to the public?

A. 1936.

———◆———

Q. What United States president dedicated the Shenandoah National Park in 1936?

A. Franklin D. Roosevelt.

———◆———

Q. Where does Virginia rank among the states in the production of tobacco products?

A. Second only to North Carolina.

———◆———

Q. What 1791 lighthouse was the first built by the U.S. government at Virginia Beach?

A. Cape Henry Lighthouse.